WHAT ARE
PEOPLE FOR?

WHAT ARE PEOPLE FOR?

ESSAYS BY

WENDELL BERRY

COUNTERPOINT
BERKELEY

Many of these essays were published in somewhat different form in the
following periodicals, magazines, anthologies, and newspapers, to which
the author and publisher wish to express their thanks: *American Poetry
Review, Antaeus, The Nation, Yale Review, Whole Earth Review, South
Dakota Review, Seneca Review, The American Authors Series* (Conflu-
ence Press), *Firmament Magazine, The Land Report, Chicago Tribune,
BioCycle, Journal of Gastonomy, Harper's Magazine,* and *The Utne
Reader.* "The Work of Local Culture" was published as a pamphlet by
the Iowa Humanities Lecture Series Board. "Writer and Region" first
appeared in *The Hudson Review,* no 1, Spring 1987.

Library of Congress Cataloging-in-Publication Data
Berry, Wendell, 1934–
    What are people for? : essays / by Wendell Berry.
        p. cm.
    ISBN: 978-1-58243-487-2
    I. Title.
AC8.B4743   1990
081—dc20   89–29848

Design by David Bullen Design
Printed in the United States of America

COUNTERPOINT
1919 Fifth Street
Berkeley, CA 94710

www.counterpointpress.com
Distributed by Publishers Group West

10 9 8 7 6 5

To Gurney Norman

CONTENTS

WHAT ARE
PEOPLE FOR?

Part I

DAMAGE

I

I have a steep wooded hillside that I wanted to be able to pasture occasionally, but it had no permanent water supply.

About halfway to the top of the slope there is a narrow bench, on which I thought I could make a small pond. I hired a man with a bulldozer to dig one. He cleared away the trees and then formed the pond, cutting into the hill on the upper side, piling the loosened dirt in a curving earthwork on the lower.

The pond appeared to be a success. Before the bulldozer quit work, water had already begun to seep in. Soon there was enough to support a few head of stock. To heal the exposed ground, I fertilized it and sowed it with grass and clover.

We had an extremely wet fall and winter, with the usual freezing and thawing. The ground grew heavy with water, and soft. The earthwork slumped; a large slice of the woods floor on the upper side slipped down into the pond.

The trouble was the familiar one: too much power, too little knowledge. The fault was mine.

I *was* careful to get expert advice. But this only exemplifies what I already knew. No expert knows everything about every place, not even everything about any place. If one's knowledge of one's whereabouts is insufficient, if one's judgment is unsound, then expert advice is of little use.

II

In general, I have used my farm carefully. It could be said, I think, that I have improved it more than I have damaged it.

My aim has been to go against its history and to repair the damage of other people. But now a part of its damage is my own.

The pond was a modest piece of work, and so the damage is not extensive. In the course of time and nature it will heal.

And yet there *is* damage—to my place, and to me. I have carried out, before my own eyes and against my intention, a part of the modern tragedy: I have made a lasting flaw in the face of the earth, for no lasting good.

Until that wound in the hillside, my place, is healed, there will be something impaired in my mind. My peace is damaged. I will not be able to forget it.

III

It used to be that I could think of art as a refuge from such troubles. From the imperfections of life, one could take refuge in the perfections of art. One could read a good poem—or better, write one.

Art was what was truly permanent, therefore what truly mattered. The rest was "but a spume that plays / Upon a ghostly paradigm of things."

I am no longer able to think that way. That is because I now live in my subject. My subject is my place in the world, and I live in my place.

There is a sense in which I no longer "go to work." If I live in my place, which is my subject, then I am "at" my work even when I am not working. It is "my" work because I cannot escape it.

If I live in my subject, then writing about it cannot "free" me of it or "get it out of my system." When I am finished writing, I can only return to what I have been writing about.

While I have been writing about it, time will have changed it. Over longer stretches of time, *I* will change it. Ultimately, it will be changed by what I write, inasmuch as I, who change my subject, am changed by what I write about it.

If I have damaged my subject, then I have damaged my art. What aspired to be whole has met damage face to face, and has come away wounded. And so it loses interest both in the anesthetic and in the purely esthetic.

It accepts the clarification of pain, and concerns itself with healing. It cultivates the scar that is the course of time and nature over damage: the landmark and mindmark that is the notation of a limit.

To lose the scar of knowledge is to renew the wound.

An art that heals and protects its subject is a geography of scars.

IV
"You never know what is enough unless you know what is more than enough."

I used to think of Blake's sentence as a justification of youthful excess. By now I know that it describes the peculiar condemnation of our species. When the road of excess has reached the palace of wisdom it is a healed wound, a long scar.

Culture preserves the map and the records of past journeys so that no generation will permanently destroy the route.

The more local and settled the culture, the better it stays put, the less the damage. It is the foreigner whose road of excess leads to a desert.

Blake gives the just proportion or control in another proverb: "No bird soars too high, if he soars with his own wings." Only when our acts are empowered with more than bodily strength do we need to think of limits.

It was no thought or word that called culture into being, but a tool or a weapon. After the stone axe we needed song and story to remember innocence, to record effect—and so to describe the limits, to say what can be done without damage.

The use only of our bodies for work or love or pleasure, or even for combat, sets us free again in the wilderness, and we exult.

But a man with a machine and inadequate culture—such as I was when I made my pond—is a pestilence. He shakes more than he can hold.

1975

HEALING

I

The grace that is the health of creatures can only be held in common.

In healing the scattered members come together.

In health the flesh is graced, the holy enters the world.

II

The task of healing is to respect oneself as a creature, no more and no less.

A creature is not a creator, and cannot be. There is only one Creation, and we are its members.

To be creative is only to have health: to keep oneself fully alive in the Creation, to keep the Creation fully alive in oneself, to see the Creation anew, to welcome one's part in it anew.

The most creative works are all strategies of this health.

Works of pride, by self-called creators, with their premium on originality, reduce the Creation to novelty—the faint surprises of minds incapable of wonder.

Pursuing originality, the would-be creator works alone. In loneliness one assumes a responsibility for oneself that one cannot fulfill.

Novelty is a new kind of loneliness.

III

There is the bad work of pride. There is also the bad work of despair—done poorly out of the failure of hope or vision.

Despair is the too-little of responsibility, as pride is the too-much.

The shoddy work of despair, the pointless work of pride, equally betray Creation. They are wastes of life.

For despair there is no forgiveness, and for pride none. Who in loneliness can forgive?

IV

Good work finds the way between pride and despair.

It graces with health. It heals with grace.

It preserves the given so that it remains a gift.

By it, we lose loneliness:

we clasp the hands of those who go before us, and the hands of those who come after us;

we enter the little circle of each other's arms,

and the larger circle of lovers whose hands are joined in a dance,

and the larger circle of all creatures, passing in and out of life, who move also in a dance, to a music so subtle and vast that no ear hears it except in fragments.

V

And by it we enter solitude, in which also we lose <u>lo</u>neliness.

Only discord can come of the attempt to share solitude.

True solitude is found in the wild places, where one is without human obligation.

One's inner voices become audible. One feels the attraction of one's most intimate sources.

In consequence, one responds more clearly to other lives. The more coherent one becomes within oneself as a creature, the more fully one enters into the communion of all creatures.

One returns from solitude laden with the gifts of circumstance.

VI

And there is no escaping that return.

From the order of nature we return to the order—and the disorder—of humanity.

From the larger circle we must go back to the smaller, the smaller within the larger and dependent on it.

One enters the larger circle by willingness to be a creature, the smaller by choosing to be a human.

And having returned from the woods, we remember with regret its restfulness. For all creatures there are in place, hence at rest.

In their most strenuous striving, sleeping and waking, dead and living, they are at rest.

In the circle of the human we are weary with striving, and are without rest.

VII

Order is the only possibility of rest.

The made order must seek the given order, and find its place in it.

The field must remember the forest, the town must remember the field, so that the wheel of life will turn, and the dying be met by the newborn.

The scattered members must be brought together.

Desire will always outreach the possible. But to fulfill the possible is to enlarge it.

The possible, fulfilled, is timely in the world, eternal in the mind.

Seeing the work that is to be done, who can help wanting to be the one to do it?

But one is afraid that there will be no rest until the work is finished and the house is in order, the farm is in order, the town is in order, and all loved ones are well.

But it is pride that lies awake in the night with its desire and its grief.

To work at this work alone is to fail. There is no help for it. Loneliness is its failure.

It is despair that sees the work failing in one's own failure.

This despair is the awkwardest pride of all.

VIII

There is finally the pride of thinking oneself without teachers.

The teachers are everywhere. What is wanted is a learner.

In ignorance is hope. If we had known the difficulty, we would not have learned even so little.

Rely on ignorance. It is ignorance the teachers will come to.

They are waiting, as they always have, beyond the edge of the light.

IX

The teachings of unsuspected teachers belong to the task, and are its hope.

The love and the work of friends and lovers belong to the task, and are its health.

Rest and rejoicing belong to the task, and are its grace.

Let tomorrow come tomorrow. Not by your will is the house carried through the night.

Order is only the possibility of rest.

1977

Part II

A REMARKABLE MAN

I

"Nate Shaw" is the pseudonym of a black farmer born in Alabama in 1885. He grew up as a field hand and sharecropper in the cotton belt. Because of his industry, ambition, and intelligence, he prospered. By the early 1930s he owned a good team of mules, good farming equipment, two automobiles; his family was well cared for; he was on the way to owning an eighty-acre farm. At that time he joined the Sharecroppers Union. He took a stand against some sheriff's deputies who had come to attach and carry off a neighbor's stock. The confrontation ended in a "shootin frolic," for which Nate Shaw was sent to prison for twelve years. He stayed the full term, refusing a parole bargain by which he would have had to leave his home country and move to Birmingham, and was released in 1945. Older, drastically reduced in means, he returned to farming, "a mule farmin man to the last," though the tractor era had come in during his absence. In March of 1971 he began to tell his story to a young white man, Theodore Rosengarten. The telling, recorded on tapes, took 120 hours; the result, much edited, is this remarkable book. Our debt to Mr. Rosengarten is large.

It is a remarkable book because Nate Shaw was a remarkable man. And it is worthwhile to try to say exactly why he was remarkable. He was not remarkable because he belonged to "the tradition of farmer-storytellers." Most farmers of Nate Shaw's generation belonged to the tradition of farmer-storytellers, and I am sure that a great many of them were good talkers indeed. Nor is he remarkable for what Mr. Rosengarten calls his "awe-

Review of Theodore Rosengarten, *All God's Dangers: The Life of Nate Shaw*, Alfred A. Knopf, 1974.

some intellectual life." The adjective seems to me overwrought, as if Mr. Rosengarten were trying to *make* Nate Shaw admirable, which is not necessary. With us, the phrase "intellectual life" suggests a life *exclusively* intellectual, a life apart from action, and Nate Shaw was remarkable because the life of his body and the life of his mind were one life. He had, obviously, a superior intelligence, but he was not a modern intellectual. His thought was not speculative or experimental; it was not an overrefined maundering among "alternatives." It was a meditation upon experience, always related to acts.

Shaw's words have the energy of passionate knowledge; he speaks as a man who has *seen*. It is characteristic of him to say, "Well, I looked into all that and seed . . . " He had no schooling; his book-learning is all described in one sentence: "I can put down on paper some little old figures but I can't add em up." But he says of the failure of his lawyer's appeal, following his sentencing for the shooting: "That was my education right there—" In a sense, it must have been. That event—his stand against the deputies and his imprisonment—was not only the great event and the turning point of his life; it was also his life's measure, its clarification or revelation. He speaks with the pressing awareness that "I understand a heap of things today more clear than I did in them days . . . " And sometimes his memories hasten and crowd him almost beyond coherence. He exclaims at one point: "O, these words brings up others and they won't wait . . . " His words are principled by his certainty that "there's nothin honorable before God but the truth."

I am troubled because Mr. Rosengarten's name appears on the book as author rather than editor, which he was, and because the book is subtitled *The Life of Nate Shaw* rather than *The Autobiography of Nate Shaw*, which it is.

More troubling is the comparison of Shaw with Faulkner, initiated by Mr. Rosengarten in his preface and followed already by several reviewers. Mr. Rosengarten commits himself to this supposed likeness with a simple-mindedness hard to believe:

"Faulkner writes about the white south; Shaw speaks about the black. Both focus on the impact of history on the family." The first sentence falsifies Shaw and Faulkner both; if there is any single truth basic to southern history, it is that there never has been a "white south" or a "black south." The second sentence is useless because, although it is at least partly true, it is probably just as true of most writers. The great difference between Shaw and Faulkner is passed over lightly indeed in the concession that one speaks and the other writes. That is a fundamental difference, and other important differences follow from that one.

The idea seems to be that until the blacks have *their* Faulkner they won't be "equal"; Mr. Rosengarten's sentences fairly sigh with relief. It is as if liberality requires us to pretend that the whites and the blacks are exactly alike in everything but color, like salt and pepper shakers. This could be agreed upon, maybe, and we could make an etiquette of ignoring our differences. But what if the differences do exist? And what if the two races are useful and necessary to each other because of their differences? And what if they have access to certain aspects of their experience and their common nationality only *through* each other? Shaw is valuable to us precisely because he is *not* like Faulkner. He is richly different.

II

Shaw's vocabulary and usage will sometimes seem strange to readers not familiar with his region and way of life, but it will never seem empty or inert. When he speaks of "correspondin" a girl or says that his son "got stout enough to accomplish a place," we have no trouble understanding what he means, and we are also aware that his words convey insight beyond the reach of conventional usage. He speaks always in reference to a real world, thoroughly experienced and understood. His words keep an almost physical hold on "what I have touched with my hands and what have touched me . . . " Surely this is the power that we have periodically sensed in what is called (vulgarly) "the vulgar tongue." It is a language under the discipline of experience, not of ideas or rules. Shaw's words, always interposed between experience and intelligence, have the exactitude of conviction, whereas the words of an analyst or theorist can have only the exactitude of definition.

In a recent issue of *Saturday Review/World*, R. Buckminster Fuller has an article called "Cutting the Metabilical Cord," which is based on a virtually unqualified assumption that humanity has begun a process of unlimited improvement by way of technological progress. "Humanity knew very little when I was young," he says. And he recalls the "skilled craftsmen" he worked with on his first jobs; these people "had vocabularies of only about 100 words, many of which were blasphemous or obscene." Thanks to radio and television, however, this lamentable ignorance has been corrected by a "historic information-education explosion and its spontaneous edifying of humans in general." This "explosion" of edification "completely changed the speech pattern of world-around humanity from that of an illiterate ignoramus to that of a scholar." These and many similar assertions culminate in a sort of Creed for Modern Times: "The great intellectual integrity of universe has cut the metabilical cord of tradition and parental authority—putting youth on its own thinking responsibility." And then occurs the essay's only note of caution, which is immediately buried beneath another avalanche of technological mysticism: the young people of 1974, "whose metabilical cord of tradition has been cut, now need a few years time to develop competence to take over the world affairs initiative, and that is exactly what universe is apparently about to do next."

It may be that Mr. Fuller's language can be put to some good use. I hope so. It could certainly be used to promote the sale of television sets. Should his jargon catch on with the public, it could also be useful to any politician whose designs required a fit of public optimism. This gobbledygook of "universe" is representative of a lot of the sub-tongues spoken now by people who lead "awesome intellectual lives." It is speech so abstract, so far removed from anybody's experience, that it is virtually out of control; *anything* can be said in it that the speaker has the foolishness or the audacity to say.

There is not a phrase in Nate Shaw's story so abstract, naive, ignorant, insipid, or tasteless as this language of Buckminster Fuller. An "uneducated" man whose speech was formed long before radio, Shaw is nevertheless well able to say whatever he thinks, and he thinks whatever he needs to think as a man of exceptional competence, both practical and moral. In moments of joy or grief, he is capable of a sort of poetry. The burden—and so the discipline—of Shaw's language is what he knows from experience. For that reason nothing he says, if correctly quoted, will ever be useful to a salesman or a political propagandist. There is not a single slogan in this book. He has no talk of "education explosions" or "metabilical cords." He does not say "Freedom now" or "Black is beautiful" or "Power to the people." He says: "My color, the colored race of people on earth, goin to shed theirselves of these slavery ways. But it takes many a trip to the river to get clean." He says: "They goin to win! They goin to win! But it's goin to take a great effort. . . . It won't come easy. Somebody got to move and remove. . . . It's goin to take thousands and millions of words, thousands and millions of steps. . . . And I hope to God that I won't be one of the slackers that would set down and refuse to labor to that end."

That is eminently responsible language. And it is deeply moving—especially when we realize that the man speaking almost in the same breath of faith, doubt, difficulty, and his own willingness to *labor* is eighty-six or -seven years old. The movement here is characteristic: the swiftly defined hope or vision or ambition, followed by the recognition of difficulty, the implication of labor. And these passages occur among *stories* that reveal the nature and the difficulty of effort and the characters of people, black and white. What this responsibility rests on is the knowledge of tragedy. Shaw's mind has dwelt upon his own limits, both cultural

and human; it has dwelt upon loss and upon solitude. Buckminster Fuller writes, "Obviously, humanity if properly cooperative and scientifically coordinated can do anything it needs
to do"—acknowledging neither the enormous ifs that cling to
"properly cooperative" nor the political portent of "scientifically coordinated." Nate Shaw, a more unified man, who can
speak of acting "with the full consent of my mind," has *done*
what he *thought*, and so he knows the solitude of the man who
acts on principle. When he "stood up against this southern way
of life," he had to stand alone; the other members of the union
fled. He knew the exultation of his stand: "That made me merry
in a way. I done what was right. . . ." But he also knew its tragedy:
"When they shot me it didn't shake me, when they arrested me it
didn't shake me. But it shook me to see my friends was but few."

If Shaw's language is never far from experience, it is also never
far from judgment, another of his qualities that will make him
useless to propagandists. The amplitude of his experience, the
energy of his intelligence, his great courage simply will not permit him to withhold his judgment. It is always working, and it
can be fierce. But the same qualities that bring it into play give it
the dignity of freedom from prejudice and special pleading. One
must assume, having no evidence but Shaw's, that he may sometimes be wrong, but it could rarely be argued that he is partial. He
is as hard on blacks as on whites. He finds good people in both
races. He knew people of both races who were partly good and
partly bad. And this intelligence of judgment aligns him with the
best men who have taken the stand he took: he knows that what
he stands for, what he asks for himself, is a human and not a racial good. He knows that white people also stand to gain from
what he has hoped to gain for himself and for his race. And he
makes a careful distinction between white men and white
money-men: "Color don't boot with the big white cats: they only
lookin for money. O, it's plain as your hand. The poor white man
and the poor black man is sittin in the same saddle today . . ."

III

Every page of this book is resonant with Shaw's intelligence, with his delight in the use of his mind. And this is a conscious delight: "I've learned many a thing that's profitable to me, and I've learned a heap that ain't profitable, but to learn anything at all is a blessin." A few pages later he says: "And I treasures what I know and I so often think about it . . ."

Similarly, his pride, his moral pride, is both an explicit theme and a quality implicit in every word. From childhood Shaw's life was governed by self-respect, love of work, pride in accomplishment, high standards for his own work and behavior. "I depends on myself to act just suchaway," he says. And: "If I has anything to do I must do all I can at it; I just feels terrible if I don't." And from the first he seems to have had an indomitable impulse to be independent: "I was dependin on the twist of my own wrist." "I was a poor young colored man but I had the strength of a man who comes to know himself." These virtues were the direct cause both of what he knew of prosperity and of what he knew of calamity. This passionate involvement of his mind and character in all his acts becomes finally the intelligence of his speech, and makes it memorable.

I do not see how anybody could consider the depth and range of Shaw's intelligence, the power, sensitivity, and precision of his speech, and doubt the superiority of this man. And yet, though Shaw knew his superiority, had carefully assembled and pondered its evidence, in a part of his mind he seems to have remained half in doubt of it. This uneasiness springs from his lack of formal education. The book has two themes—counter-themes—that will show what I am talking about.

Shaw's pages are full of evidence that he was a farmer, not just by necessity of birth and condition, but by choice as well. It is luck, of course, when one loves to do what one has to do. But the fact remains that Shaw loved to farm. He had an exultant interest in it. He says so directly, and there is an implicit joy in all the passages about his work. And yet his lack of education obviously nags at him, forcing him to suspect that his farmer's life was his limitation: "My boyhood days was my hidin place. I didn't have no right to no education whatever. I was handicapped and handicapped like a dog." And he says that the educational opportunities that followed the civil rights movement "brought light out of darkness."

I assent wholeheartedly to the first theme and at least in principle to the second. But I feel an uncertainty, perhaps a conflict. This is one of the rare instances when Shaw exemplifies a problem that he does not illuminate. A powerful superstition of modern life is that people and conditions are improved inevitably by education. Within the limits of the life he lived, and of the evidence he gives, this proposition certainly seems to apply to Shaw: he would have been less at the mercy of employers, landlords, and creditors, for example, if he had been able to read. Or he might, maybe, have been a better farmer if he had had some schooling. Suppositions of this sort are blind, of course, but one has to suppose also that if Nate Shaw had been well enough educated, he might long ago have become a spokesman, perhaps for his race, perhaps for small farmers of his sort of both races.

My skepticism on this question comes from two directions. On one hand, I am aware of a powerful cultural inheritance—part of which Nate Shaw's story represents and now joins—that rises from long before the civil rights movement or even emancipation, and that is perhaps not so much light out of darkness as light *in* darkness. A fact too easy to ignore in our climate of conventional pity for the "disadvantaged" is that Nate Shaw is not *potentially* admirable; he is admirable *as he is*. And to assume that he could have become so admirable without drawing on a strong, sustaining culture would be as fantastical as to pity him in light of what he might have been.

On the other hand, I am aware that such a man as Nate Shaw stands outside the notice, much less the aim, of the education system. From the standpoint of our social mainstream, the idea of a

well-educated small farmer, of any race, has long been a contra-
diction in terms, and so of course our school systems can hardly
be said to tolerate any such possibility. The purpose of education
with us, like the purpose of society with us, has been, and is, to
get away from the small farm—indeed, from the small everything. The purpose of education has been to prepare people to
"take their places" in an industrial society, the assumption being
that all small economic units are obsolete. And the superstition
of education assumes that this "place in society" is "up." "Up" is
the direction from small to big. Education is the way up. The
popular aim of education is to put everybody "on top." Well, I
think I hardly need to document the consequent pushing and
trampling and kicking in the face. My point is that if the reader
joins Nate Shaw in wishing that he might have been educated, he
cannot safely assume that he is wishing only for an improved
Nate Shaw; he may be wishing for a different kind of human
creature altogether. With education—given his intelligence, his
strong character, his local fidelities, and a good deal of luck—
Shaw *might* have become a well-educated small farmer. But he
might also have become a "farm expert," and thus the natural enemy of his economic class. Or he might have become another big
cat, "only lookin for money."

What I am working toward is a definition of this book as a
burden. It *is* a burden—in addition, of course, to being multifar-
iously informative and delightful. At first I thought the burden
would be Shaw's indictment of racism and economic oppression.
His testimony on these subjects is fierce and eloquent—and burdening too, Lord knows. But on these subjects Shaw is only one
of many witnesses. His response to those conditions—his *stand*
—is what is rare. And he made his stand "with the full consent of
his mind." I have called it an act of principle, but that is to give it
the shallowest definition. It was the action of his character: it was
prepared by his whole life up to that time. It was, as much as himself, native to his place in the world.

And that brings me in sight of what I want to say: Shaw burdens us with his character. Not just with his testimony, or with his actions, but with his *character*, in the fullest possible sense of that word. Here is a superior man who never went to school! What a trial that ought to be for us, whose public falsehoods, betrayals of trust, aggressions, injustices, and imminent catastrophes are now almost exclusively the work of the college bred. What a trial, in fact, that *is* for us, and how guilty it proves us: we think it ordinary to spend twelve or sixteen or twenty years of a person's life and many thousands of public dollars on "education"—and not a dime or a thought on character. Of course, it is preposterous to suppose that character could be cultivated by any sort of public program. Persons of character are not public products. They are made by local cultures, local responsibilities. That we have so few such persons does not suggest that we ought to start character workshops in the schools. It does suggest that "up" may be the wrong direction.

IV

This is the book of a black man; Shaw keeps a deliberate faith with his responsibilities as a spokesman for his race. But it is also, almost as constantly, a farmer's book. When he speaks as a farmer, Shaw steps beyond the limits of his racial experience— and enters into another kind of tragedy.

Shaw's book is full of the folk-agrarianism that undoubtedly lay behind the agrarianism of Jefferson, that survived in small farmers and even field hands and sharecroppers of both races until well into this century. It is the agrarianism of "forty acres and a mule," the frustrated hope of emancipated slaves, but nevertheless one of the few intelligent and decent social aspirations that our history has produced. Shaw's book, by either his fault or his editor's, does not say how this tradition came to him or who his teachers might have been. Evidently it did not come to him from his father, whom Shaw held in some contempt as a free man with slavery ways, who "couldn't learn nothin from his experience." But however it came to him, Shaw did inherit the aspiration, the attitudes, and the know-how of this old agrarianism, and his exemplification of it is one of the values of his book.

His understanding of the meaning of land ownership is complex and responsible, as is his understanding of the relationship between property and labor. He knows that for men such as himself, ability is futile if it has no title to land; it simply comes under the control of whoever does own the land. He knows the dangers implicit in a man's willingness to own more land than he can work. It is exactly because of this knowledge that Shaw cannot be said to speak only about the experience of black people; the notion belittles him. When he "stood up" to oppose his neighbor's—and ultimately his own—dispossession, he had generations of his people's history behind him, and he knew it. But in that act an important strand of white people's history also reached one of its culminations, and in a different way he knew that.

Shaw's standing up stated and clarified a principle that his life worked out in detail. His ideal was independence, and that carried his mind to fundamentals. He was not a "consumer." The necessities of life were of no negligible importance to him. Provisioning, with him, was not just a duty, but a source of excitement, a matter of pride. He knew that his hopes depended on a sound domestic economy. He raised a garden, kept a milk cow or two, fed his own meat hogs and so reduced his family's dependence on the stores. "I was saving myself a little money at the end of each year, gettin a footin to where I wouldn't have to ask nobody for nothin."

As a consequence, he began "to rise up," not to "the top," but to a sufficiency of ability and goods. There are exultant passages in which he tells of buying his own mules, new wagons, and harness. Like thousands of men of his generation, white and black, his great pride was in his teams and in his ability as a teamster. Some of the finest parts of his book are about his mules. Memories of the good ones carry him away: "O, my mules just granted me all the pleasure I needed, to see what I had and how they moved."

He had a fierce loyalty to his own country and to the investment of his own labor in it. He would not consider going north or to the city. He would not even use city water, though at the end of his life a new water line went right by his door: "I ain't livin in no city. I ain't too lazy to step outside and help myself . . . and the water ain't fit for slops." For his people, he is mistrustful of welfare ("since the government been givin em a handdown," he says of certain people he knows, "they wouldn't mind the flies off their faces") and of the city jobs that leave "the possession and the use of the earth to the white man." His loyalty to his place made him a conservationist, and one of his most indignant outbursts is against polluters.

By the time of his imprisonment, Shaw's values were solidly proven in his life. He was a self-respecting and an accomplished man, and he was by no means the only one who knew it. Twelve years later, when he was released from prison, he had not only lost much that he had earned, but he had become an anachronism as well. A new kind of farming had come in: "I knowed as much about mule farmin as ary man in this country. But when they brought in tractors, that lost me." By the time he tells his story, he realizes that for his deepest knowledge—the knowledge that made him a man in his own sight—he has no heir. An antique collector has come to buy his tools: "There's people decorates their homes with things that belong to the past."

Mr. Rosengarten says in his preface that Shaw's language is "enriched here and there by words not found in the dictionary." I collected several examples of what I assume he is talking about. All that I found *are* in the dictionary; Mr. Rosengarten failed to recognize them because he was unfamiliar either with Shaw's dialect or with farming. He spells hames "haines," backband "backbend" and "backhand," Duroc Jersey "Dew Rock Jersey."

He has Shaw say that "the old horse went *backin* on off," when he obviously could only have meant *racking*.

This is more than a trifling editorial inadvertence. It is the up-cropping in Shaw's own sentences of the cultural discontinuity that troubled his old age. Instead of coming in its live meaning to the ears of his children's children, his story has come to print through the hands of people who do not know the names of the substantial things that ruled his life, much less the use or the cultural importance of those things. The book that has saved him for readers, most of whom also will not know these things, thus shows how near we have come to losing him.

1975

HARRY CAUDILL IN
THE CUMBERLANDS

On July 15, 1965, a friend then living in Hazard gave me my first look at the strip mines of eastern Kentucky. The strip miners at that time were less "regulated" than they are now, and under the auspices of the notorious "broad form deed" they frequently mined without compensation to the surface owners. The result was wreckage on an unprecedented scale: the "overburden" was simply pushed off the coal seam onto the mountainside to go wherever gravity would take it; houses with their families still in them were carried down the slopes by landslides, wells polluted by acid from the exposed coal seams, streams poisoned and choked with rubble; and the whole establishment of the people on the land was treated simply as so much more "overburden." There could have been no better demonstration of the motives and the moral character of the business of energy.

That night we attended a meeting of the Appalachian Group to Save the Land and the People in the courthouse at Hindman. The occasion of the meeting was the arrest the day before of Dan Gibson, a respected farmer and lay preacher who had gone onto the mountain with a gun and turned back the strip miners' bulldozers. He was acting on behalf of a younger member of his family then in the service; he was past eighty years old, he said, and had nothing to lose by dying. Thirteen state police, a sheriff, and two deputies had been sent to rescue the thus-threatened free enterprise system, and a shooting was averted only by the intervention of several members of the Group, who persuaded the police

Review of Harry M. Caudill, *The Mountain, the Miner, and the Lord*, The University Press of Kentucky, 1980.

to allow *them* to take the old man before the local magistrate. The magistrate, an employee of the mining company, placed Mr. Gibson under a bond of $2,000. He did not stay long in jail, but the whole affair was so clearly an outrage as to give a vivid sense of injury, identity, and purpose to the assemblage in the Knott County courtroom the following night.

The meeting was called to order, the events of the preceding day were described by various witnesses, and then Harry Caudill was called upon and came to the front of the room. I had read *Night Comes to the Cumberlands* perhaps two years before, and was full of respect for it, but until then I had never seen its author. I do not expect to forget him as I saw and heard him that night. He spoke with the eloquence of resolute intelligence and with the moral passion of a lawyer who understood and venerated the traditions of justice.

They are destroying our land under our very households, he said. They are going to drive us out as the white men drove out the Indians. And they have prepared no reservation to send us to. The law has been viciously used against us, and it must be changed. We have been made fools of for sixty years, and now at last maybe we are going to do something about it. And he spoke of "the gleeful yahoos who are destroying the world, and the mindless oafs who abet them." It was a statement in the great tradition that includes the Declaration of Independence and the Bill of Rights. And it was a statement, moreover, to which Harry Caudill had dedicated his life; he had outlined it fully in *Night Comes to the Cumberlands*, and in the coming years he would elaborate it in other books, in many speeches, articles, and public letters. The statement—the indictment, the plea for justice—has, I think, remained essentially the same, but the *case* has been relentlessly enlarged by the gathering of evidence, by thought, reading, and research. For twenty years his has been an able public voice recalling us to what, after all, we claim as "our" principles.

In that same twenty years, hundreds of spokesmen in the same cause have come and gone, hundreds of protests have flared and burned out, hundreds of "concerned" officials have made wages or made hay and gone on. Harry Caudill is one of the few who have endured. As recently as January 5, 1981, a long letter to the editor of the *Louisville Courier-Journal* set his argument yet again before the people of his native state. A few quotations from it will suggest the quality both of the argument and of the man.

First, the indictment:

> The state taxes coal in the ground at the rate of 1/10 cent per $100 of value—a mere 315th part of the rate levied on houses and farms. The severance tax is 4½ percent as compared to rates ranging from 12½ percent to 30 percent in the western fields, and most of it returns to the coalfields to build and repair coal roads. The coal industry enjoys low taxes, public esteem, political power, and immense profits. The people generally carry all the burdens growing out of ruined roads, silted rivers and lakes, polluted water, inadequate housing, poor schools, and low health standards.

And then he calls the roll of the beneficiaries of this curious welfare state:

> . . . Kentucky River Coal, Occidental Oil, Gulf Oil, Ford Motor, Neufinanze AG (of Lichtenstein), KyCoGo Corporation, Stearns Coal and Lumber, U.S. Steel, Royal Dutch Shell, National Steel, Koppers Corporation, Columbia Gas, Equitable Gas, Big Sandy Corporation, Tennessee Valley Authority, Harvard University, Southern Railway, Diamond Shamrock, International Harvester, Howell Oil Company . . .

And he concludes with the obvious question:

> Why should Kentucky be the nation's leading coal-producing state if all we get out of it is crippled and dead miners, silted streams and lakes, torn up roads, uprooted forests and holes in the ground?

Harry Caudill's frustration has been that this question has never been satisfactorily answered. His triumph is that he has kept asking it, has kept making the same good sense, invoking the same principles, measuring by the same high standards year after year. The passion of his intelligence has been to know what he is talking about, to condescend to no occasion, to indulge in none of the easy pangs of "disillusionment." What has kept him going?

Not, I think, his sense of justice or his capacity for moral outrage—or not only those things. A sense of justice, though essential, grows pale and cynical when it stands too long alone in the face of overpowering injustice. And moral outrage, by itself, finally turns intelligence into rant. To explain the endurance of Harry Caudill, it is necessary to look deeper than his principles.

It is a fact, and an understandable one, I think, that many would-be defenders of the land and people of eastern Kentucky have felt both to be extremely uncongenial. The region is, after all, part of a "national sacrifice area," and has been so considered and so treated by governments and corporations for well over half a century. The marks of the ruin of both land and people are everywhere evident, are inescapable, and to anyone at all disposed to regret them they tend to be depressing. The first article on strip mining I ever read began by saying how delighted the writer had been to leave Hazard, Kentucky, where he had served a protracted journalistic term of, I believe, one week. Harry Caudill, by contrast, can write: "I had the good fortune to be born in 1922 in Letcher County, Kentucky." He did not come there, then, to serve justice. He has been there because he has belonged there; the land and people for whom he has spoken are his own. Because he got his law degree and went home with it, his mind has never made the expedient separation of knowledge from value that has enabled so much industrial pillage, but has known with feeling and so has served with devotion—a possibility long disregarded by modern educators, who believe despite overwhelming evidence to the contrary that education alone, "objective knowledge," can produce beneficent results.

Another thing. As anybody knows who ever got within earshot of this man, Harry Caudill is a superb storyteller. A lecture, public or private, on the industrialization of the coal fields is apt to be followed by a string of wonderful tales, each reminding him of another, all riding on a current of exuberant delight and laughter. And this telling and the accompanying laughter do not come, I think, as escape or relief from the oppressive realities of the lecture, but come from the same life, the same long concentration on the same region and people.

And so this book, *The Mountain, the Miner, and the Lord*, which would be welcome enough by itself, is particularly welcome because it is a significant part, until now missing from the printed record, of Harry Caudill's statement about his region. It is not "something different," but belongs innately to the twenty years' work that began with *Night Comes to the Cumberlands* and is a part of its explanation.

In the preface, valuable in itself as a remarkably compact, incisive historical essay on his region, Mr. Caudill tells how these stories came to him: "I practiced law within a mile of my birthplace for twenty-eight years and saw and talked to a daily procession of people. . . . I tried to afford them a good listener." Or that is the way most of the stories came; elsewhere in the book he makes us aware that some of them, or some parts of them, were learned in the years of his childhood and youth. It is evident in places (and is nearly everywhere supposable) that the stories were not heard all together, as they stand here, but were collected in scraps from various other rememberers and tellers and pieced together over the years like quilts.

"These tales," he writes, "are intended to show how the cultural layers were formed and a people fashioned." And they do that, or help to do it. They show again and again, for example, how the parade of national history and power has impinged on the region: the frontier, the Civil War and its various successors, Prohibition and the continuing federal excitement over moonshine, corporations, unions, welfare, et cetera. They show also the influence of cultural inheritance, topography, geography, poor farming, and the oppressions of coal.

But they also do—and are—more than that. They spring, as perhaps the best stories always have, from the ancient fascination with human extremity, from the tendency, apparently native to us all, to remember and tell and tell again the extravagances of human vice and virtue, comedy and tragedy. This book contains a number of examples of the sort of outrageous wisdom that passes endlessly through the talk of rural communities:

> One woman ain't hardly enough fer a man if he is any account a-tall.

> The worst thing that can happen to a man is to need a pistol and not have it!

There are tales of justice, public and private, heartwarming or hair-raising. There are the inevitable chapters of the region's history of violence. Best of all, to me, is "The Straight Shooter," a political biography of one Fess Whitaker: I don't know how it could be better told.

This book, I fear, is doomed to be classed by those who live by such classification as "folk" material. But they had better be careful. It is, for one thing, very much a lawyer's book. Harry Caudill is master of an art of storytelling that I think could rightly be called "legal," for it has been practiced by country lawyers for many generations. Its distinction and distinctive humor lie in the understanding of the tendency of legal rhetoric to overpower its occasions:

> Thereupon he towered above Collins like a high priest at some holy rite and poured forth a generous libation of buttermilk upon the judge's pate, shoulders, and other parts.

For another thing, these stories—though they have to do with people who by a certain destructive condescension have been called "folk"—are the native properties of an able, cultivated, accomplished, powerful, and decent mind.

1981

A FEW WORDS
IN FAVOR OF
EDWARD ABBEY

Reading through a sizable gathering of reviews of Edward Abbey's books, as I have lately done, one becomes increasingly aware of the extent to which this writer is seen as a problem by people who are, or who think they are, on his side. The problem, evidently, is that he will not stay in line. No sooner has a label been stuck to his back by a somewhat hesitant well-wisher than he runs beneath a low limb and scrapes it off. To the consternation of the "committed" reviewer, he is not a conservationist or an environmentalist or a boxable ist of any other kind; he keeps on showing up as Edward Abbey, a horse of another color, and one that requires some care to appreciate.

He is a problem, apparently, even to some of his defenders, who have an uncontrollable itch to apologize for him: "Well, he did *say* that. But we mustn't take him altogether seriously. He is only trying to shock us into paying attention." Don't we all remember from our freshman English class how important it is to get the reader's attention?

Some environmentalist reviewers see Mr. Abbey as a direct threat to their cause—a man embarrassingly prejudiced or radical or unruly. Not a typical review, but one representative of a certain kind of feeling about Edward Abbey, was Dennis Drabelle's attack on *Down the River* in *The Nation* of May 1, 1982. Mr. Drabelle accused Mr. Abbey of elitism, iconoclasm, arrogance, and xenophobia; he found that Mr. Abbey's "immense popularity among environmentalists is puzzling" and observed that "many of his attitudes give aid and comfort to the enemies of conservation."

Edward Abbey is, of course, a mortal requiring criticism, and I would not attempt to argue otherwise. He undoubtedly has some of the faults he has been accused of having, and maybe some others that have not been discovered yet. What I *would* argue is that attacks on him such as that of Mr. Drabelle are based on misreading, and that the misreading is based on the assumption that Mr. Abbey is both a lesser man and a lesser writer than he in fact is.

Mr. Drabelle and others like him assume that Mr. Abbey is an environmentalist—and hence that they, as other environmentalists, have a right to expect him to perform as their tool. They further assume that if he does not so perform, they have a proprietary right to complain. They would like, in effect, to brand him an outcast and an enemy of their movement and to enforce their judgment against him by warning people away from his books. Why should environmentalists want to read a writer whose immense popularity among them is puzzling?

Such assumptions, I think, rest on yet another assumption that is more important and more needful of attention: namely, that our environmental problems are the result of bad policies, bad political decisions, and that, therefore, our salvation lies in winning unbelievers to the righteous political side. If all those assumptions were true, then I suppose that the objections of Mr. Drabelle would be sustainable: Mr. Abbey's obstreperous traits would be as unsuitable in him as in any other political lobbyist. Those assumptions, however, are false.

Mr. Abbey is not an environmentalist. He is, certainly, a defender of some things that environmentalists defend, but he does not write merely in defense of what we call "the environment." Our environmental problems, moreover, are not, at root, political; they are cultural. As Edward Abbey knows and has been telling us, our country is not being destroyed by bad politics; it is being destroyed by a bad way of life. Bad politics is merely another result. To see that the problem is far more than political is to return to reality, and a look at reality permits us to see, for example, what Mr. Abbey's alleged xenophobia amounts to.

The instance of xenophobia cited by Mr. Drabelle occurs on page seventeen of *Down the River*, where Mr. Abbey proposes that our Mexican border should be closed to immigration. If we permit unlimited immigration, he says, before long "the social, political, economic life of the United States will be reduced to the level of life in Juarez. Guadalajara. Mexico City. San Salvador. Haiti. India. To a common peneplain of overcrowding, squalor, misery, oppression, torture, and hate." That is certainly not a liberal statement. It expresses "contempt for other societies," just as Mr. Drabelle says it does. It is, moreover, a fine example of the exuberantly opinionated Abbey statement that raises the hackles of readers like Mr. Drabelle—as it is probably intended to do. But before we dismiss it for its tone of "churlish hauteur," we had better ask if there is any truth in it.

And there is some truth in it. As the context plainly shows, this sentence is saying something just as critical of ourselves as of the other countries mentioned. Whatever the justice of the "contempt for other societies," the contempt for the society of the United States, which is made explicit in the next paragraph, is fearfully just: "We are slaves in the sense that we depend for our daily survival upon an expand-or-expire agro-industrial empire—a crackpot machine—that the specialists cannot comprehend and the managers cannot manage. Which is, furthermore, devouring world resources at an exponential rate. We are, most of us, dependent employees"—a statement that is daily verified by the daily news. And its truth exposes the ruthless paradox of Mexican immigration: Mexicans cross the border because our way of life is extravagant; because our way of life is extravagant, we have no place for them—or won't have for very long. A generous immigration policy would be contradicted by our fundamentally ungenerous way of life. Mr. Abbey assumes that before talking about generosity we must talk about carrying capacity, and he is correct. The ability to be generous is finally limited by the availability of supplies.

The next question, then, must be: If he is going to write about immigration, why doesn't he do it in a sober, informed, logical manner? The answer, I am afraid, will not suit some advocates of sobriety, information, and logic: He *can* write in a sober, informed, logical manner—if he *wants* to. And why does he sometimes not want to? Because it is not in his character to want to all the time. With Mr. Abbey, character is given, or it takes, a certain precedence, and that precedence makes him a writer and a man of a different kind—and probably a better kind—than the practitioner of mere sobriety, information, and logic.

In classifying Mr. Abbey as an environmentalist, Mr. Drabelle is implicitly requiring him to be sober, informed, and logical. And there is nothing illogical about Mr. Drabelle's discomfort when his call for an environmentalist was answered by a man of character, somewhat unruly, who apparently did not know that an environmentalist was expected. That, I think, is Mr. Abbey's problem with many of his detractors. He is advertised as an environmentalist. They *want* him to be an environmentalist. And who shows up but this *character*, who writes beautifully some of the time, who argues some of the time with great eloquence and power, but who some of the time offers opinions that appear to be only his own uncertified prejudices, and who some of the time, even in the midst of serious discussion, makes *jokes*.

If Mr. Abbey is not an environmentalist, what is he? He is, I think, at least in the essays, an autobiographer. He may be writing on one or another of what are now called environmental issues, but he remains Edward Abbey, speaking as and for himself, fighting, literally, for dear life. This is important, for if he is writing as an autobiographer, he *cannot* be writing as an environmentalist—or as a special ist of any other kind. As an autobiographer, his work is self-defense; as a conservationist, it is to conserve himself as a human being. But this is self-defense and self-conservation of the largest and noblest kind, for Mr. Abbey understands that to defend and conserve oneself as a human being in the fullest, truest sense, one must defend and conserve many others and much else. What would be the hope of being personally whole in a dismembered society, or personally healthy in a land scalped, scraped, eroded, and poisoned, or personally free in a land entirely controlled by the government, or personally enlightened in an age illuminated only by TV? Edward Abbey is fighting on a much broader front than that of any "movement." He is fighting for the survival not only of nature, but of *human* nature, of culture, as only our heritage of works and hopes can define it. He is, in short, a traditionalist—as he has said himself, expecting, perhaps, not to be believed.

Here the example of Thoreau becomes pertinent. My essay may seem on the verge of becoming very conventional now, for one of the strongest of contemporary conventions is that of comparing to Thoreau every writer who has been as far out of the house as the mailbox. But I do not intend to say that Mr. Abbey writes like Thoreau, for I do not think he does, but only that their *cases* are similar. Thoreau has been adopted by the American environment movement as a figurehead; he is customarily quoted and invoked as if he were in some simple way a forerunner of environmentalism. This is possible, obviously, only because Thoreau has been dead since 1862. Thoreau was an environmentalist in exactly the sense that Edward Abbey is: he was for some things that environmentalists are for. And in his own time he was just as much of an embarrassment to movements, just as uncongenial to the group spirit, as Edward Abbey is, and for the same reasons: he was working as an autobiographer, and his great effort was to conserve himself as a human being in the best and fullest sense. As a political activist, he was a poor excuse. What was the political value of his forlorn, solitary taxpayer's revolt against the Mexican War? What was politic about his defense of John Brown or his insistence that abolitionists should free the *wage* slaves of Massachusetts? Who could trust the diplomacy of a man who would pray:

Great God, I ask thee for no other pelf
Than that I may not disappoint myself;
. . . .
And next in value, which thy kindness lends,
That I may greatly disappoint my friends . . .

The trouble, then, with Mr. Abbey—a trouble, I confess, that I am disposed to like—is that he speaks insistently as himself. In any piece of his, we are apt to have to deal with all of him, caprices and prejudices included. He does not simply *submit* to our criticism, as does any author who publishes; he virtually demands it. And so his defenders, it seems to me, are obliged to take him seriously, to assume that he generally means what he says, and, instead of apologizing for him, to acknowledge that he is not always right or always fair—which, of course, he is not. Who is? For me, part of the experience of reading him has always been, at certain points, that of arguing with him.

My defense of him begins with the fact that I *want* him to argue with, as I want to argue with Thoreau. If we value these men and their work, we are compelled to acknowledge that such writers submit to standards raised, though not necessarily made, by themselves. We, with our standards, must take them as they come, defend ourselves against them if we can, agree with them if we must. If we want to avail ourselves of the considerable usefulness and the considerable pleasure of Edward Abbey, we will have to like him as he is. If we cannot like him as he is, then we will have to ignore him, if we can. My own notion is that he is going to become harder to ignore, and for good reasons, not the least of which is that the military-industrial state is working as hard as it can to prove him right.

It seems virtually certain that no reader can read much of Mr. Abbey without finding some insult to something that he or she approves of. Mr. Abbey is very hard, for instance, on "movements"—the more solemn and sacred they are, the more they tempt his ridicule. He is a great irreverencer of sacred cows. There is not one sacred cow of the sizable herd still on the range that he has left ungoosed. He makes his rounds as unerringly as the local artificial inseminator. This is one of his leitmotifs. He gets around to them all. His are glancing blows, mainly, delivered on the run, with a weapon no more lethal than his middle finger. The following is fairly typical:

> The essays in *Down the River* are meant to serve as antidotes to despair. Despair leads to boredom, electronic games, computer hacking, poetry and other bad habits.

That example is appropriate here because it passingly gooses one of my own sacred cows: poetry. I am inclined to be tickled rather than bothered by Mr. Abbey's way with consecrated bovines, and this instance does not stop me long—though I do pause to think that *I*, anyhow, would not equate poetry with electronic pastimes. But if one is proposing to take Mr. Abbey seriously, one finally must stop and deal with such matters. *Am* I, then, a defender of "poetry"? The answer, inevitably, is no; I am a defender of *some poems*. Any human product or activity that humans defend as a category becomes, by that very fact, a sacred cow—in need, by the same fact, of an occasional goosing.

Some instances of this activity are funnier than others, and readers will certainly disagree as to the funniness of any given instance. But whatever one's opinion, in particular or in general, of Mr. Abbey's blasphemies against sacred cows, one should be wary of the assumption that they are merely humorous or (as has been suggested) merely "image-making" stunts calculated to sell articles to magazines. They are, I think, gestures or reflexes of his independence, his refusal to act as a spokesman or a property of any group or movement, however righteous. This refusal keeps the real dimension and gravity of our problems visible to him, and keeps him from falling for easy answers. You never hear Mr. Abbey proposing that the fulfillment of this or that public program, or the achievement of the aims of this or that movement, or the "liberation" of this or that group, will save us. The absence in him of such propositions is one of his qualities, and it is a welcome relief.

The funniest and the best of these assaults are the several that are launched head-on against the most exalted of all the modern sacred cows: the self. Mr. Abbey's most endearing virtue as an autobiographer is his ability to stand aside from himself and recount his most outrageous and self-embarrassing goof-ups, with a bemused and gleeful curiosity, as if they were the accomplishments not merely of somebody else, but of an altogether different kind of creature. I envy him that. It is, of course, a high achievement. How absurd we humans in fact are! How misapplied is our self-admiration—as we can readily see by observing other self-admiring humans! How richly just and healthful is self-ridicule! And yet how few of us are capable of it. I certainly find it hard. My own goof-ups seem to me to have received merciless publicity when my wife has found out about them.

Because Mr. Abbey is so humorous and unflinching an autobiographer, he knows better than to be uncritical about anything human. That is why he holds sacred cows in no reverence. And it is at least partly why his reverence for nature is authentic: he does not go to nature to seek himself or flatter himself, nor does he speak of nature to display his sensitivity. He is understandably reluctant to reveal himself as a religious man, but the fact occasionally appears plainly enough: "It seems clear at last that our love for the natural world—Nature—is the only means by which we can requite God's obvious love for it."

The most interesting brief example of Abbey humor that I remember is his epigram on "gun control" in his essay "The Right to Arms." "If guns are outlawed," he says, "only the government will have guns." That sentence, of course, is a parody of the "gun lobby" bumper sticker: "If guns are outlawed, only outlaws will have guns." It seems at first glance only another example of sacred cow goosing—howbeit an unusually clever one, for it gooses *both* sacred cows involved in this conflict: the idea that, because guns are used in murders, they should be "controlled" by the government, and the idea that the Second Amendment to the Bill of Rights confers a liberty that is merely personal. Mr. Abbey's sentence, masquerading as an instance of his well-known "iconoclasm," slices through the distractions of the controversy to the historical and constitutional roots of the issue. The sentence is, in fact, an excellent gloss on the word "militia" in the Second Amendment. And so what might appear at first to be merely an "iconoclastic" joke at the expense of two public factions becomes, on examination, the expression of a respectable political fear and an honorable political philosophy, a statement that the authors of our Constitution would have recognized and welcomed. The epigram is thus a product of wit of the highest order, richer than the excellent little essay that contains it.

Humor, in Mr. Abbey's work, is a function of his outrage, and is therefore always answering to necessity. Without his humor, his outrage would be intolerable—as, without his outrage, his humor would often be shallow or self-exploitive. The indispensable work of his humor, as I see it, is that it keeps bringing the whole man into the job of work. Often, the humor is not so much a property of the argument at hand as it is a property of the stance from which the argument issues.

Mr. Abbey writes as a man who has taken a stand. He is an *interested* writer. This exposes him to the charge of being prejudiced, and prejudiced he certainly is. He is prejudiced against tyranny over both humanity and nature. He is prejudiced against sacred cows, the favorite pets of tyrants. He is prejudiced in favor of democracy and freedom. He is prejudiced in favor of an equitable and settled domestic life. He is prejudiced in favor of the wild creatures and their wild habitats. He is prejudiced in favor of charitable relations between humanity and nature. He has other prejudices too, but I believe that those are the main ones. All of his prejudices, major and minor, identify him as he is, not as any reader would have him be. Because he speaks as himself, he does not represent any group, but he *stands* for all of us.

He is, I think, one of the great defenders of the idea of property.

His novel *Fire on the Mountain* is a moving, eloquent statement on behalf of the personal proprietorship of land: *proper* property. And this espousal of the cause of the private landowners, the small farmers and small ranchers, is evident throughout his work. But his advocacy of that kind of property is balanced by his advocacy of another kind: public property, not as "government land," but as wild land, wild property, which, belonging to nobody, belongs to everybody, including the wild creatures native to it. He understands better than anyone I know the likelihood that one kind of property is not safe without the other. He understands, that is, the natural enmity of tyranny and wilderness. "Robin Hood, not King Arthur," he says, "is the real hero of English legend."

You cannot lose your land and remain free; if you keep your land, you cannot be enslaved. That old feeling began to work its way toward public principle in our country at about the time of the Stamp Act. Mr. Abbey inherits it fully. He understands it both consciously and instinctively. This, and not nature love, I think, is the real motive of his outrage. His great fear is the fear of dispossession.

But his interest is not just in *landed* property. His enterprise is the defense of all that properly belongs to us, including all those thoughts and works and hopes that we inherit from our culture. His work abounds in anti-intellectual jokes (he is not going to run with *that* pack, either), but no one can read him attentively without realizing that he has read well and widely. His love for Bach is virtually a theme of his work. His outrage often vents itself in outrageousness, and yet it is the outrage of a cultivated man—that is why it is valuable to us, and why it is interesting.

He is a cultivated man. And he is a splendid writer. Readers who allow themselves to be distracted by his jokes at their or our or his expense cheat themselves out of a treasure. The xenophobic remark that so angers Mr. Drabelle, for example, occurs in an essay, "Down the River with Henry Thoreau," which is an excellent piece of writing—entertaining, funny some of the time, aboundingly alive and alert, variously interesting, diversely instructive. The river is the Green, in Utah; the occasion was a boat trip by Mr. Abbey and five of his friends in November 1980. During the trip he read *Walden* for the first time since his school days. This subjection of a human product to "the prehuman sanity of the desert" is characteristic of Mr. Abbey's work, the result of one of his soundest instincts. His account of the trip is, at once, a travelogue, a descriptive catalog of natural sights and wonders, and a literary essay. It is an essay in the literal sense: a trial. Mr. Abbey tries himself against Thoreau and Thoreau against himself; he tries himself and Thoreau against the river; he tries himself and Thoreau and the river against modern times, and vice versa. The essay looks almost capriciously informal, but only a highly accomplished and knowledgeable writer could have written it. It is, among all else, a fine literary essay—such a reading of *Walden* as Thoreau would have wanted, not by the faceless automaton of current academic "scholarship," but by a man outdoors, whose character is in every sentence he writes.

I don't know that that essay, good as it is, is outstanding among the many that Mr. Abbey has written. I chose to speak of it because Mr. Drabelle chose to speak of it, and because I think it represents its author well enough. It exhibits one of his paramount virtues as a writer, a virtue paramount in every writer who has it: he is always interesting. I have read, I believe, all of his books except one, and I do not remember being bored by any of them. One reason is the great speed and activity of his pages; a page of his, picked at random, is likely, I believe, to have an unusual number of changes of subject, and to cover an unusual amount of ground. Another reason is that he does not oversimplify either himself or, despite his predilection for one-liners, his subject. Another reason is his humor, the various forms of which keep breaking through the surface in unexpected places, like wet-weather springs.

But the quality in him that I most prize, the one that removes him from the company of the writers I respect and puts him in the smaller company of the writers I love, is that he sees the gravity, the great danger, of the predicament we are now in, he tells it unswervingly, and he defends unflinchingly the heritage and the qualities that may preserve us. I read him, that is to say, for consolation, for the comfort of being told the truth. There is no longer any honest way to deny that a way of living that our leaders continue to praise is destroying all that our country is and all the best that it means. We are living even now among punishments and ruins. For those who know this, Edward Abbey's books will remain an indispensable solace. His essays, and his novels too, *are* "antidotes to despair." For those who think that a few more laws will enable us to go on safely as we are going, he will remain—and good for him!—a pain in the neck.

1985

WALLACE STEGNER
AND THE GREAT
COMMUNITY

In the spring of 1958 I received notice that I had been given a Stegner Fellowship for the next school year at Stanford University. I assumed, properly enough, that I was going to be dealing with people my own age who would know a great deal more than I did. Clearly, I needed to prepare myself.

My wife and new daughter and I were staying in Lexington, Kentucky, that summer, and I decided that I would read the works of Wallace Stegner. The only thing I had read by him up to then was *Field Guide to the Western Birds*, published by Ballantine in a collection called *New Short Novels 2*. In those days I assumed that anything that interested me had already interested everybody else, and so I was surprised to find that the university library yielded only his first novel, *Remembering Laughter*, and his second book of stories, *The City of the Living*. I found a copy of the first short story collection, *The Women on the Wall*, in a used book store.

My reading of those three books is still clear and immediate to me, perhaps because my uneasiness about going to Stanford had sharpened my wits. I thought *Remembering Laughter* a perfect little novel, clean and swift and assured, and I can still feel the weight of the disaster in it. As the would-be author of a first novel myself, I envied it and was intimidated by it. I saw plainly that this man, when he was perhaps my age, had known how to write, and that he had known how much better than I did.

Because I had no ambition to write short stories, I read *The*

Women on the Wall and *The City of the Living* more dispassionately. By then I had read a good many short stories. Besides the ones scattered in textbooks and anthologies, I had read Hemingway's in the Modern Library collection and Faulkner's *Collected Stories*. But I had read those mainly, I think, as a reader—without asking how they had been made. *The Women on the Wall* and *The City of the Living* were the first collections of stories by one writer that I read asking that question, seeing how an able workman made use of a form.

And so Wallace Stegner became my teacher before I ever laid eyes on him, and he was already teaching me in a way that I have come to see as characteristic of him: by bestowing a kindness that implied an expectation, and by setting an example.

It has been twenty-seven years since 1958, and I am no longer certain what I expected him to be. All I am sure of is that I did not expect him to be as he was when he took over the writing seminar at the start of the winter quarter. Perhaps, since he taught at a great university and had written many books, I expected him to be magisterial. Perhaps I expected him to display the indisputable field marks of Literary Genius. Or perhaps I expected a dogmatist of some sort, for I remember that he had a reputation with some former writing students still around as a stickler for grammar—as if *grammar* had anything to do with *art*.

The man himself, it turned out, was something altogether different, and a great deal better. When I was asked to write about him as a teacher, I had the feeling that I was expected to tell anecdotes of memorable classroom performances. But that is not what I have to tell. As a teacher, as I knew him, he had none of the performer in him. When he spoke to the class, the class felt spoken to. You did not feel that he was glancing at himself.

What struck me first about him was the way he looked. He was, and still is, an extraordinarily handsome man. And unlike many writers and professors, he dressed with care and looked good in his clothes. I don't mean that he was a dandy; he was as far from that as he was from being a performer. His was a neatness, one felt, that had to do with respect, for himself and for others.

But just as striking, just as unexpected, was the way he understated his role as teacher. I think that he is naturally a reticent man, not given to self-revelation or self-advertisement, and for years I assumed that his reticence in the classroom was merely a part of his character. But as I have come to know him better, have read him more, and have thought more about him, I have changed my mind. I am sure that character had something to do with it, but it seems to me now that his stance and manner in the classroom were the results of an accurate and generous understanding of his situation as teacher and of ours as students. The best explanation may be in these sentences from his essay "The Book and the Great Community":

> Thought is neither instant nor noisy. . . . It thrives best in solitude, in quiet, and in the company of the past, the great community of recorded human experience. That recorded experience is essential whether one hopes to re-assert some aspect of it, or attack it.

The community here is that of "recorded human experience," not the Pantheon of Great Writers. It is immense and diverse, more like the Library of Congress than the Harvard Five-Foot Shelf. But it does include the great writers. It is bewildering both in its amplitude and in the eminence of some of its members. A teacher leading his students to the entrance to that community, as would-be contributors to it, must know that both he and they are coming into the possibility of error. The teacher may make mistakes about the students; the students may make much more serious ones about themselves. He is leading them, moreover, to a community, not to some singular stump or rostrum from which he will declare the Truth.

I think, then, that when Mr. Stegner sat with us at the long table in the Jones Room of the Stanford Library, he felt that a certain modesty and a certain discretion were in order. He did not speak as though he confused any utterance of his with the earthquake that one afternoon gently shook us while we talked.

There must have been about twenty of us in the class, and among its members were Ernest Gaines, Ken Kesey, and Nancy Packer. Nancy, I think, was the oldest of us. She had read a great deal, talked well, and was useful to us all. But as a group we had a good deal to say, and Mr. Stegner would let us say it. He would read a piece of somebody's work and then sit back, sometimes with a cigar, listening attentively while we had our say.

One sunny afternoon he read us a piece of work of his own—a chapter, I think, from *All the Little Live Things*—and then graciously paid attention to all we said to him about it. I remember that I made an extensive comment myself, and I am tempted to wish I could remember what I said. Probably I should be glad to have forgotten. I would be glad, anyhow, to know that he has forgotten.

He had his say too, of course. He commended generously where commendation was due. He was a good encourager when encouragement was needed. And, more important, he was a willing dealer with problems, even little problems, even—yes— problems of grammar. That is, he gave good practical help.

He did not adopt the pose or use the tactics of the authoritarian teacher, and yet one felt his authority. I am not talking, of course, about institutional authority, which must be asserted to be felt, and which he did not assert. We felt in him, rather, the authority of authentic membership in the great community, of one who had thought and worked in solitude, in quiet, in the company of the past—an authority that would be destroyed in being asserted.

It was this implicit authority in him that most impressed me during my time at Stanford. That and an expectation implicit in his dealings with me, that perhaps was not conscious with him, but which I felt keenly. At one time in the midst of my fellowship year I thought (mistakenly, it turned out) that I had finished the novel I was working on, and I could not see clearly what I ought to do next. For a while, paralyzed in my confusion, I was not able to write anything. And I remember both my embarrassment, for I felt that Mr. Stegner expected me to be at work, and how paltry, in light of his expectation, my excuses appeared in my own eyes. That was, maybe, my definitive encounter with the hardest truth that a writer—or any other worker—can learn: that, to all practical purposes, excuses are not available.

Mr. Stegner's teaching, then, as I have come to see it, was as important for what it did not do as for what it did. One thing he did not do was encourage us too much. If we wrote well, he said so. But he did not abet any suspicions we may have had that we were highly accomplished writers or that we were ever going to be highly accomplished. In this, I think, he respected the past, for he was better acquainted with the art of writing than we were and knew better than we did how much we had to learn. But he was being respectful of us too. He did not want to mislead us or help us to mislead ourselves. He did not say what he had not considered or did not mean. He did not deal in greetings at the beginnings of great careers.

He did not pontificate or indoctrinate or evangelize. We were not expected to become Stegnerians. None of us could have doubted that he wanted us to know and think and write as well as we possibly could. But no specific recipe or best way was recommended. The emphasis was on workmanship. What we were asked to be concerned with was the job of work at hand, what one or another of us had done or attempted to do. Our teacher was a writer, he too was at work on what he had chosen to do; he would help us if he could.

And so what I began by calling reticence—at some risk, for it is not a fashionable virtue now—finally declares itself as courtesy toward both past and future: courtesy toward the art of writing, which needs to be carefully learned and generously passed on; and courtesy toward us, who as young writers needed all the help we could get, but needed also to be left to our own ways.

In his conversations with Richard Etulain, there is a passage in which Mr. Stegner names several of his old students, speaks of their accomplishments, and then says, "I try not to take credit for any of that." In the mouths of some people, that statement would not be trustworthy; in the mouths of some it would contradict itself. Coming from Mr. Stegner, it is trustworthy, for in fact he has not been a taker of credit. The fellows *have* been left to their ways. They have come, benefited as they were able, and left free of obligation.

My bet, however, is that, by the fellows and other students, Wallace Stegner is given a great deal more credit than he would be comfortable in taking. The first fellowships were given in 1946. By 1971, when Mr. Stegner retired from teaching, there had been about a hundred of them, and the list of fellows contains a good many names that do it credit: Evan S. Connell, Dan Jacobson, Hannah Green, Eugene Burdick, Edward Abbey, Thomas McGuane, Ken Gangemi, Tillie Olsen, Robert Stone, Jim Houston, Larry McMurtry, Ernest Gaines, James Baker Hall, Gurney Norman, Ed McClanahan, Peter Beagle, Nancy Huddleston Packer, Max Apple, Blanche Boyd, Judith Rascoe, Max Crawford, Robin White, Merrill Joan Gerber, Charlotte Painter, Al Young, Raymond Carver, William Wiegand, William Kittredge.

My bet is that every one of those people owes something to Wallace Stegner. My further bet is that most of them, maybe years after their participation in the seminar, have been surprised by some recognition of what and how much they owe. And yet I know that a teacher is right in trying not to take credit for his students. The fellows, one assumes, must have learned something from attending the seminars given by Mr. Stegner, Richard Scowcroft, and other teachers. But they must have learned something too from coming to California and living there for a year. They must have learned something from one another, and from other people they came to know while they were there. They must have learned something from the books they read while they were there. How would you sort all that out, for the hundred fellows and the hundreds of others who sat in the Jones Room from 1946 to 1971, and make a precise estimate of the influence of one teacher? Obviously, you cannot. As thousands of faculty committees have found out, "teacher evaluation" is a hopeless business. There is, thank God, no teacher-meter, and there never is going to be one. A teacher's major contribution may pop out anonymously in the life of some ex-student's grandchild. A teacher, finally, has nothing to go on but faith, a student nothing to offer in return but testimony.

What I have to testify is that, although I do not think that Mr. Stegner thinks of himself as my teacher, my awareness of him as a teacher has grown over the years, and I think myself more than ever his student. And this has to do with the changes that have happened in me since my time at Stanford.

In those days I assumed, as my education had prepared me to assume, that I was going to follow a literary career that would lead me far from home. I assumed that I would teach (and write) in a university in a large city, and in fact I did so for a while. And then my family and I returned to my native county in Kentucky. That is, I became, in both habitat and subject, what is called a "regional writer."

There are, of course, problems in being a regional writer. If one is regional only in subject, then there is a temptation—and an abundance of precedent—for becoming a sort of industrialist of letters, mining one's province for whatever can be got out of it in the way of "raw material" for stories and novels. I would argue that it has been possible for such writers to write so exploitively, condescendingly, and contemptuously of their regions and their people as virtually to prepare the way for worse exploitation by their colleagues in other industries: if it's a god-forsaken boondocks full of ignorant hillbillies, or a god-forsaken desert populated by a few culturally deprived ranchers, why *not* strip-mine it?

On the other hand, if one both lives and writes in one's region, one becomes aware of good reasons to be more watchful and more careful. It was not until I began the struggle to live and write in my region that I began to be aware of Wallace Stegner as a writer struggling to live and write in *his* region—something I would never have done, I think, had I chosen to live in San Francisco or New York. Or at least his struggle would not have meant so much, would not have been so instructive and reassuring to me, had I lived in one of those places. In *Wolf Willow* and then in *The Sound of Mountain Water*, I saw him dealing head-on with the problems of the history and the literary history of the West, the challenges and flaws and threats of those histories, and the possible meanings and uses of his own history as a westerner. And of course, once one sees this effort in some of his work, one begins to see it in the rest. One sees him becoming a new kind of writer: one who not only writes about his region but also does his best to protect it, by writing and in other ways, from its would-be exploiters and destroyers.

As a regional writer he seems to me exemplary. He has worked strenuously to know his region. He has been not just a student of its history, but one of its historians. There is an instructive humility in his studentship as a historian of the West. It is hard to imagine Hemingway researching and writing a history of Michigan or Africa; to him, as to many writers now, history was immediate experience. To Mr. Stegner, it is also memory. He has the care and the scrupulousness of one who understands remembering as a duty, and who therefore understands historical insight and honesty as duties. He has endeavored to understand the differences of his region from other regions and also from its own pipe dreams and fantasies of itself. He has never condescended to his region—an impossibility, since he has so profoundly understood himself as a part of it. He has not dealt in the quaint, the fantastical, or the picturesque. And, above all, he has written well. He is a highly accomplished and an extremely versatile writer. One of the pleasures in reading him is to see how many kinds of writing he has done well. He does not allow suppositions about the homeliness or provinciality of his subject to qualify or limit his own powers. He writes as intelligently about cowboys as about historians and literary critics.

He is a re-readable writer. One reads out of interest or curiosity to see how the story or the argument or the explanation will play itself out. One can re-read, I think, only to be surprised. If re-reading does not yield surprises, one does not continue. Not long ago, when I re-read "Genesis," the long story in *Wolf Willow*, I was surprised by the excellence of the artistry, its clarity and crispness, the cleanness of movement. It is a story by a man who learned about work and hardship, weather and country, from experience, but who has also thought well about them, and has read well. More recently, re-reading some of the essays, I was surprised by the way they spoke, amplifying themselves, to the time and experience added to me since I read them last.

He is, then, a regional writer who has escaped the evils of regional-ism. And he has escaped, as well, the evils of idiosyncrasy. He has been a writer whose work has not exhausted literary possibility, but has made it, opened it up. Younger writers of the West, I would think, would find it possible to build on his work directly. And younger writers of other regions, I know, will find it illustrative of possibilities, a measure of excellence, and a source of comfort.

I have been using the adjective "regional" as if I am not aware of the antipathy attached to it in some literary circles. I am using it that way because I feel strongly the need for the sort of regional identification and commitment that is exemplified in Mr. Stegner's work. But I am, of course, inescapably aware of the scorn with which that identification and commitment are frequently met. Mr. Stegner himself cites a typical instance in his conversations with Richard Etulain: the *New York Times*, he says, called him "the Dean of Western Writers"—and got his name wrong.

The adjective "western," as all regional writers will understand, would have been dismissive even if the name had been correctly given. This is the regionalism of New York, which will use the West, indeed depend on it, but not care for it. And this regionalism is opposed and corrected by writing that is authentically and faithfully regional.

In the face of this metropolitan regionalism which has so far been under no constraint to see itself as such, and which has condescended to and exploited all other regions, Mr. Stegner has taken his stand as a westerner and has produced work that seems to me not only excellent, but indispensable as well. And what I most respect in him is that in all the years of his effort he has not stooped to the self-promotion endemic to the literary regionalism of New York. He has represented himself solely by his writings and his acts of citizenship. In a self-exploiting, world-exploiting age, this is a high and admirable accomplishment in itself.

1985

A POEM OF
DIFFICULT HOPE

A poem by Hayden Carruth that I have returned to many times is the one entitled "On Being Asked to Write a Poem Against the War in Vietnam." The poem, in the guise of a refusal, responds directly to the invitation:

Well I have and in fact
more than one and I'll
tell you this too

I wrote one against
Algeria that nightmare
and another against

Korea and another
against the one
I was in

and I don't remember
how many against
the three

when I was a boy
Abyssinia Spain and
Harlan County

and not one
breath was restored
to one

shattered throat
mans womans or childs
not one not

one
but death went on and on
never looking aside

except now and then like a child
with a furtive half-smile
to make sure I was noticing.

This poem obviously does not need explaining, and yet it presents a problem, first of understanding and then of criticism, that is unusual and difficult. I read the poem a good many times, I confess, before I was able to say why it interested me—before, that is, I was able to acknowledge the extent to which I am involved in and with its problem. The problem that the poet appears to be replying to is this: Why do something that you suspect, with reason, will do no good? And the poem appears to give, or to be, a negative reply: There is no use in doing it.

But after this refusal is given, the completed poem begins to imply another, more important and more formidable, question: What is the use of *saying* "There is no use"? The use, I think, depends on to whom and on how this denial is given.

In the first place, the distinguishing characteristic of absolute despair is silence. There is a world of difference between the person who, believing that there is no use, says so to himself or to no one and the person who says it aloud to someone else. A person who marks his trail into despair remembers hope—and thus has hope, even if only a little. But if he speaks of despair, he must know it, and he must speak as one who knows it. Speech about despair raises, the same as speech about anything else, the question of authenticity or honesty: How do we know he knows what he is talking about? And so we must, after all, examine the language and the making of this very plain and clear poem.

The thing we notice immediately is that the poem comes to us in the sound of a voice speaking. And here it is necessary to insist on a distinction between verse written in "spoken" (as opposed to "literary") English, which may or may not have the qualities that lift verse into poetry, and verse that has the sound of a voice speaking, which does not necessarily have to be written in "spoken" English. The sound of a voice speaking, I think, often does have the power of lifting verse into poetry, for it is the power that authenticates feeling. Hayden Carruth is a master in poetry of the speaking voice, whether the voice is his own or someone else's. This mastery is not a matter of effects contrived out of diction and phraseology; I don't think it can be done that way. It is the result of technical skill so perfect and assured that it does not pause to admire itself, and therefore calls little attention to itself. The poem at hand is technically masterful, and its mastery, like that of a good cup or spoon, is unobtrusive; if not consciously looked for, it is not seen. But if we are looking, we see that the voice immediately characterizes the speaker. This voice is colloquial and cranky, absolutely direct, informed by feeling that has a history, and it has the courage to begin at full force. We know all this by the end of the first line, which gives us nothing but the quality of the voice: "Well I have and in fact . . ." It is a line superbly cocked toward the declaration it leads into.

This declaration is a single sentence, unpunctuated except for the period at the end. The absence of punctuation tends to collapse the several grammatical units into a single thrust of syntax through the divisions of lines and stanzas. We have only to look at Hayden Carruth's prose to suspect how much his poetic mastery is a mastery of syntax. Here is one of his prose sentences: "Verlaine, who in his life must be accounted among the most miserable of men, nevertheless had a steady, forthright mind." This is an unpretentious, useful sentence; it is also a masterful one, though again it has the modesty of authentic mastery. Only when we consciously examine it do we comment to ourselves on its balance, elegance, and exactitude. But when we say the sentence aloud or write it down, we *feel* all this immediately, and more besides. We feel also its wholeness as sense and as rhythmic pattern, and we feel the propriety of its length. The sentence's power is in its wholeness, its coherence, and it is a felt and a hear-able wholeness. The sentence is sensible in both senses, as a sentence should be.

In this poem, Mr. Carruth has imposed upon the long breath of his powerful syntax the measures of lines and sentences, forcing it toward the heightened tension and the exacting stresses and halts of music. Thus we get the great beauty and pathos of the cadence "not one not // one," which written or spoken as prose is flat and uninteresting. The poem gets its power, its coherence and momentum, from syntax, and it gets its precise emotional articulateness from the rhythmic divisions of line and stanza. This balance of power and exactitude authenticates the voice, which authenticates the statement. We feel that the poet knows what he is talking about because he is taking such palpable care to tell us exactly. The technical skill of this poem is the signature of the poet's concern to say what he has to say and to have it understood.

But we are now brought back more forcibly than ever to the odd and difficult question we started with: What is the use of saying "There is no use"? Obviously, the poet has not fallen into the silence of perfect despair, for he is speaking; and he is not talking only to himself, for he has published his poem. A use is thus clearly implied, but what is it? We can amplify the question a little to make it more precise, but in doing so we increase its apparent oddity: Why has this poet expended so much skill and care to tell us there is no use in doing what he has already done a number of times and is now, in fact, doing again? "Is this a trick?" one is tempted to ask, for it is impossible not to see that the poet, in the act of refusing to write a poem against the war, has written one.

It is, to say the least, an unusually complex protest poem. It is a poem that complicates our understanding of what political protest is and means. We fret and ponder over it so because in its astonishing simplicity it has placed us directly in the presence of one of the bewilderments of our history and one of the mysteries of our nature.

We are living in the most destructive and, hence, the most stupid period of the history of our species. The list of its undeniable abominations is long and hardly bearable. And these abominations are *not* balanced or compensated or atoned for by the list, endlessly reiterated, of our scientific achievements. Some people are moved, now and again, to deplore one abomination or another. Others—and Hayden Carruth is one—deplore the whole list and its causes. Much protest is naive; it expects quick, visible improvement and despairs and gives up when such improvement does not come. Protesters who hold out longer have perhaps understood that success is not the proper goal. If protest depended on success, there would be little protest of any durability or significance. History simply affords too little evidence that anyone's individual protest is of any use. Protest that endures, I think, is moved by a hope far more modest than that of public success: namely, the hope of preserving qualities in one's own heart and spirit that would be destroyed by acquiescence.

A protest poem, then, had better confront not only the impossibility of restoring what has already been destroyed, but also the likelihood that it will be unable to prevent further destruction. This is simply one of the practicalities of political dissent and protest. And Mr. Carruth's poem takes up this practicality and makes music of it. He makes a protest poem that understands carefully the enforced, the inescapable, modesty of protest poems. And so his poem becomes necessarily more than a protest poem: it is also a lamentation for the dead who could not be saved, and for the poet who could not save them.

But something more is involved that is even harder to talk about because it is only slightly understandable, and that is the part that suffering plays in the economy of the spirit. It seems plain that the voice of our despair defines our hope exactly; it seems, indeed, that we cannot know of hope without knowing of despair, just as we know joy precisely to the extent that we know sorrow. Our culture contains much evidence that this is so, but one says so outright with some fear of giving justification to those dogmatic and violent people who undertake to do good by causing suffering. Is it necessary, as some appear to have supposed, to *cultivate* despair and sorrow in order to know hope and joy? No, for there will always be enough despair and sorrow. And what might have been the spiritual economy of Eden, when there was no knowledge of despair and sorrow? We don't need to worry about that.

What we do need to worry about is the possibility that we will be reduced, in the face of the enormities of our time, to silence or to mere protest. Mr. Carruth's protest poem is a poem against reduction. On its face, it protests—yet again—the reduction of the world, but its source is a profound instinct of resistance against the reduction of the poet and the man who is the poet. By its wonderfully sufficient artistry, the poem preserves the poet's wholeness of heart in the face of his despair. And it shows us how to do so as well. If we would help if we could, we will help when we can.

1990

STYLE AND GRACE

Works of art participate in our lives; we are not just distant observers of *their* lives. They are in conversation among themselves and with us. This is a part of the description of human life; we do the way we do partly because of things that have been said to us by works of art, and because of things that we have said in reply.

For a long time, I have been in conversation with Hemingway's "Big Two-hearted River," and with myself *about* "Big Two-hearted River." I have read the story many times, always with affection and gratitude, noticing and naming its virtues, and always seeing clearly in imagination the landscape and all the events of Nick Adams's restorative fishing trip. It is this clarity with which Hemingway speaks his story into the reader's imagination that is his great and characterizing virtue:

> The river made no sound. It was too fast and smooth. . . . Nick looked down the river at the trout rising. . . . As far down the long stretch as he could see, the trout were rising, making circles all down the surface of the water, as though it were starting to rain.

There is a moving courage in this plainness, freeing details, refusing clutter.

But that is not what my conversation with this story has been about. It has been about the ending, when Nick has fished down the river to where it leaves the sunlight and enters a heavily wooded swamp. At that point Nick turns back because "in the fast deep water, in the half light, the fishing would be tragic."

The story ends: "There were plenty of days coming when he could fish the swamp." I assume that such days were indeed coming, but they do not come in this story. And I have asked myself what it means that the story ends where it does, and what Hemingway meant by "tragic."

So far, I have been unable to believe that he meant the word literally. The swamp seems to be a place where one might hook big fish and then lose them, but tragedy is not a name for the loss of fish. Or it may be that Nick fears that fishing in the swamp would make him sad, a dark swamp inevitably suggesting or symbolizing what is mysterious or bewildering. But the correct name for such sadness (in anticipation, at least) is melancholy, not tragedy. It is hard to escape the feeling that Hemingway uses "tragic" more seriously than a casual speaker would use "awful" or "terrible," but not much more. If he means the word seriously, then he is talking about a tragedy that he knows about but the reader does not.

At any rate, the story receives a challenge at the end that it does not accept: it refuses to go into the dark swamp. I think that what it calls "tragic" is really messiness or unclarity, and that it refuses out of a craftsmanly fastidiousness; it will not relinquish the clarity of its realization of the light and the river and the open-water fishing. It is a fine story, on its terms, but its terms are straitly limited.

Similarly, the burned town and countryside at the beginning might have been felt as tragic, suggestive as they are of the war damage in Nick's past—but they are felt, in fact, only as a kind of cleansing away of all that is past, leaving Nick in isolation: "He felt he had left everything behind." That sentence sets the story in its bounds: it cannot be tragic because it is about a solitary man in an unmemoried time. So far as we can learn from the story itself, the man comes from nowhere, knows and is known by nobody, and is going nowhere—nowhere, at least, that he cannot see in full daylight.

"Big Two-hearted River" seems to me, then, to be a triumph of style in its pure or purifying sense: the ability to isolate those parts of experience of which one can confidently take charge. It does not go into dark swamps because it does not know how it will act when it gets there. The problem with style of this kind is that it is severely reductive of both humanity and nature: the fisherman is divided from history and bewilderment, the river from its darkness. Like the similarly reductive technical and professional specializations of our time, this style minimizes to avoid mystery. It deals with what it does not understand by leaving it out.

Lately, my conversation with "Big Two-hearted River" has been joined and a good deal clarified by Norman Maclean's long story "A River Runs Through It," also a story about fishing, not so neat or self-contained as Hemingway's, but just as fine, on its own terms, and far more moving.

Fishing, in Mr. Maclean's story, is not a rite of solitary purification, a leaving of everything behind, but a rite of companionship. It is a tragic rite because of our inevitable failure to understand each other; and it is a triumphant rite because we can love completely without understanding. Fishing, here, is understood as an art, and as such it is emblematic of all that makes us companions with one another, joins us to nature, and joins the generations together. This is the connective power of culture. Sometimes it works, sometimes it fails; when it fails, it fails into tragedy, but here it is a tragedy that confirms the completeness, and indeed the immortality, of love.

Though the river of "A River Runs Through It" is the Big Blackfoot, which, so far as we are told, enters no swamp, the whole story takes place in a dark swamp of sorts: the unresolvable bewilderment of human conflict and affection and loss. The style is confident enough, for Mr. Maclean accepts fully the storyteller's need to speak wholeheartedly however partial his understanding, but it is not pure or self-protective. It is a style vulnerable to bewilderment, mystery, and tragedy—and a style, therefore, that is open to grace.

This story is profoundly and elatedly religious—though it is

untainted by the doctrinal arrogance and the witless piety that
often taint "religion." Reading it, we are not allowed to forget
that we are dealing with immortal principles and affections, and
with the lives of immortal souls. "In our family," the first sentence reads, "there was no clear line between religion and fly fishing." And one is inclined at first to take that as a little family joke.
The sentence states, however, the author's conviction of the dou-
bleness, the essential mysteriousness, of our experience, which
presides over the story to the end and gives it imaginative force of
the highest kind.

The theme of fly fishing and (or as) religion is developed mas-
terfully and with exuberant humor in the first few pages, which
give the story its terms and its characters, its settled fate and its
redemption. These pages sketch out the apprenticeship served by
the writer and his younger brother, Paul, to their father, who was
a Presbyterian minister and a fly fisherman:

> As a Scot and a Presbyterian, my father believed that man by nature
> was a mess and had fallen from an original state of grace. . . . I never
> knew whether he believed God was a mathematician but he certainly
> believed God could count and that only by picking up God's rhythms
> were we able to regain power and beauty.

"Our father's art" of fly fishing, then, is seen as a way of recovering
God's rhythms and attaining grace—no easy task, for "if you
have never picked up a fly rod before, you will soon find it fac-
tually and theologically true that man by nature is a damn mess."
Before he is "redeemed," "it is natural for man to try to attain
power without recovering grace." There are sentences that we
celebrate, reading them, because they are themselves celebrations of their own exact insight: "Power comes not from power
everywhere, but from knowing where to put it on." The boys' father believed that "all good things . . . come by grace and grace
comes by art and art does not come easy."

By the end of page six, not only have these connections been
made between fishing and religion, art and grace, but attention

has also been brought to focus on Paul, the brother, who we have learned is a superb fly fisherman and a compulsive gambler. By the end of page eight we know also that he has a high temper, that he is inflexibly self-ruled, and that he is a street fighter. The story by then has its direction, which is as unbending as Paul's character. It is a story of the relentlessness of tragedy, and it is told with the relentlessness of the grace that comes by art. The story is painful, and it causes one to read on, rejoicing, to the end.

This is tragedy pretty much in the old Greek sense: a story of calamity and loss, which arrive implacably, which one sees coming and cannot prevent. But the relentlessness of the tragedy is redeemed by the persistence of grace. The entrances of grace come at moments of connection of man and fish and river and light and word and human love and divine love. If we see Paul drunk, defeated, jailed, and finally beaten to death, we also see him in glory. In the passage that follows, the writer has sat down to watch his brother fish. Paul has swum out through dangerous water to a rock and climbed up on it and begun casting. There is no minimizing here:

> Below him was the multitudinous river, and, where the rock had parted it around him, big-grained vapor rose. The mini-molecules of water left in the wake of his line made momentary loops of gossamer. . . . The spray emanating from him was finer-grained still and enclosed him in a halo of himself. The halo of himself was always there and always disappearing, as if he were candlelight flickering about three inches from himself. The images of himself and his line kept disappearing into the rising vapors of the river, which continually circled to the tops of the cliffs where, after becoming a wreath in the wind, they became rays of the sun.

The story is not in that, of course; that is only a glimpse that the story affords of the truest identity of the man it is about. The story is about the failure of the man to live up to his own grace, his own beauty and power, about the father's failure to be able to help, and about the writer's failure as his brother's keeper. And yet it is this glimpse and others like it that give the tragedy and the story their redemption and make possible the painful and triumphant affirmation at the end. This Paul, who failed, was yet a man who had learned the art of participating in grace. After his death, his brother and his father spoke of him, acknowledging their failure to help and to understand. The father asked:

"Are you sure you have told me everything you know about his death?". . . I said, "Everything." "It's not much, is it?" "No," I replied, "but you can love completely without complete understanding." "That I have known and preached," my father said. . . .

"I've said I've told you all I know. If you push me far enough, all I really know is that he was a fine fisherman."

"You know more than that," my father said. "He was beautiful."

This story's fierce triumph of grace over tragedy is possible, the story "springs and sings," because of what I earlier called its vulnerability. Another way of saying this is that it does not achieve—because it does not attempt—literary purity. Nor does one feel, as one reads, that Mr. Maclean is telling the story out of literary ambition; he tells it, rather, because he takes an unutterable joy in telling it and therefore *has* to tell it. The story admits grace because it admits mystery. It admits mystery by admitting the artistically unaccountable. It could not have been written if it had demanded to consist only of what was understood or understandable, or what was entirely comprehensible in its terms. "Something within fishermen," the writer admits, "tries to make fishing into a world perfect and apart." But this story refuses that sort of perfection. It never forgets that it is a fragment of a larger pattern that it does not contain. It never forgets that it occurs in the world and in love.

I will not, I hope, be taken to be downgrading the literary art or literary value. This story is the work of a writer who has mastered his art, and I am fully aware that it would not be appreciable otherwise. I am only trying to make a distinction between two literary attitudes and their manifestation in styles.

Hemingway's art, in "Big Two-hearted River," seems to me an art determined by its style. This style, like a victorious general, imposes its terms on its subject. We are meant always to be conscious of the art, and to be conscious of it as a feat of style.

Mr. Maclean's, in contrast, seems to me a used, rather than an exhibited, art, one that ultimately subjects itself to its subject. It is an art not like that of the bullfighter, which is public, all to be observed, but instead is modest, solitary, somewhat secretive—used, like fishing, to catch what cannot be seen.

1988

WRITER AND REGION

I first read *Huckleberry Finn* when I was a young boy. My great-grandmother's copy was in the bookcase in my grandparents' living room in Port Royal, Kentucky. It was the Webster edition, with E. W. Kemble's illustrations. My mother may have told me that it was a classic, but I did not *know* that it was, for I had no understanding of that category, and I did not read books because they were classics. I don't remember starting to read *Huckleberry Finn*, or how many times I read it; I can only testify that it is a book that is, to me, literally familiar: involved in my family life.

I can say too that I "got a lot out of it." From early in my childhood I was not what was known as a good boy. My badness was that I was headstrong and did not respond positively to institutions. School and Sunday school and church were prisons to me. I loved being out of them, and I did not behave well in them. *Huckleberry Finn* gave me a comforting sense of precedent, and it refined my awareness of the open, outdoor world that my "badness" tended toward.

That is to say that *Huckleberry Finn* made my boyhood imaginable to me in a way that it otherwise would not have been. And later, it helped to make my grandfather's boyhood in Port Royal imaginable to me. Still later, when I had come to some knowledge of literature and history, I saw that that old green book had, fairly early, made imaginable to me my family's life as inhabitants of the great river system to which we, like Mark Twain, belonged. The world my grandfather had grown up in, in the eighties and nineties, was not greatly changed from the world of Mark Twain's boyhood in the thirties and forties. And the vestiges of that world had not entirely passed away by the time of my own boyhood in the thirties and forties of the next century.

My point is that *Huckleberry Finn* is about a world I know, or knew, which it both taught me about and taught me to imagine. That it did this before I could have known that it was doing so, and certainly before anybody told me to expect it to do so, suggests its greatness to me more forcibly than any critical assessment I have ever read. It is called a great American book; I think of it, because I have so experienced it, as a transfiguring regional book.

As a boy resentful of enclosures, I think I felt immediately the great beauty, the great liberation, at first so fearful to him, of the passage in Chapter 1 when Huck, in a movement that happens over and over in his book, escapes the strictures of the evangelical Miss Watson and, before he even leaves the house, comes into the presence of the country:

> By-and-by they fetched the niggers in and had prayers, and then everybody was off to bed. I went up to my room with a piece of candle and put it on the table. Then I set down in a chair by the window and tried to think of something cheerful, but it warn't no use. I felt so lonesome I most wished I was dead. The stars was shining, and the leaves rustled in the woods ever so mournful; and I heard an owl, away off, who-whooing about somebody that was dead, and a whippoorwill and a dog crying about somebody that was going to die; and the wind was trying to whisper something to me and I couldn't make out what it was, and so it made the cold shivers run over me.

It is a fearful liberation because the country, so recently settled by white people, is already both haunted and threatened. But the liberation is nevertheless authentic, both for Huck and for the place and the people he speaks for. In the building and summoning rhythm of his catalog of the night sounds, in the sudden realization (his and ours) of the equality of his voice to his subject, we feel a young intelligence breaking the confines of convention and expectation to confront the world itself: the night, the woods, and eventually the river and all it would lead to.

By now we can see the kinship, in this respect, between Huck's voice and earlier ones to the east. We feel the same sort of outbreak as we read:

> When I wrote the following pages, or rather the bulk of them, I lived alone, in the woods, a mile from any neighbor, in a house which I had built myself, on the shore of Walden Pond, in Concord, Massachusetts, and earned my living by the work of my hands only.

That was thirty years before *Huckleberry Finn*. The voice is certainly more cultivated, more adult, more reticent, but the compulsion to get *out* is the same.

And a year after that we hear:

> I loaf and invite my soul,
> I lean and loaf at ease . . . observing a spear of summer grass.

And we literally *see* the outbreak here as Whitman's line grows long and prehensile to include the objects and acts of a country's life that had not been included in verse before.

But Huck's voice is both fresher and historically more improbable than those. There is something miraculous about it. It is not Mark Twain's voice. It is the voice, we can only say, of a great genius named Huckleberry Finn, who inhabited a somewhat lesser genius named Mark Twain, who inhabited a frustrated businessman named Samuel Clemens. And Huck speaks of and for and as his place, the gathering place of the continent's inland waters. His is a voice governed always by the need to flow, to move outward.

It seems miraculous also that this voice should have risen suddenly out of the practice of "comic journalism," a genre amusing enough sometimes, but extremely limited, now hard to read and impossible to need. It was this way of writing that gave us what I understand as regional*ism*: work that is ostentatiously provincial, condescending, and exploitive. That *Huckleberry Finn* starts from there is evident from its first paragraph. The wonder is that within three pages the genius of the book is fully revealed, and it is a regional genius that for 220 pages (in the Library of America edition) remains untainted by regionalism. The voice is sublimely confident of its own adequacy to its own necessities, its eloquence. Throughout those pages the book never condescends to its characters or its subject; it never glances over its shoulder at literary opinion; it never fears for its reputation in any "center of culture." It reposes, like Eliot's Chinese jar, moving and still, at the center of its own occasión.

I should add too that the outbreak or upwelling of this voice, impulsive and freedom-bent as it is, is not disorderly. The freeing of Huck's voice is not a feat of power. The voice is enabled by an economy and a sense of pace that are infallible, and innately formal.

That the book fails toward the end (in the sixty-seven pages, to be exact, that follow the reappearance of Tom Sawyer) is pretty generally acknowledged. It does not fail exactly into the vice that is called regionalism, though its failure may have influenced or licensed the regionalism that followed; rather, it fails into a curious frivolity. It has been all along a story of escape. A runaway slave is an escaper, and Huck is deeply implicated, finally by his deliberate choice, in Jim's escape; but he is making his own escape as well, from Miss Watson's indoor piety. After Tom reenters the story, these authentic escapes culminate in a bogus one: the freeing of a slave who, as Tom knows, has already been freed. It is as though Mark Twain has recovered authorship of the book from Huck Finn at this point—only to discover that he does not know how to write it.

Then occurs the wounding and recovery of Tom and the surprising entrance of his Aunt Polly who, true to her character, clears things up in no time—a delightful scene; there is wonderful writing in the book right through to the end. But Mark Twain is not yet done with his theme of escape. The book ends with Huck's determination to "light out for the Territory" to escape being adopted and "sivilized" by Tom's Aunt Sally. And here, I think, we are left face-to-face with a flaw in Mark Twain's character that is also a flaw in our national character, a flaw in our history, and a flaw in much of our literature.

As I have said, Huck's point about Miss Watson is well taken and well made. There is an extremity, an enclosure, of conventional piety and propriety that needs to be escaped, and a part of the business of young people is to escape it. But this point, having been made once, does not need to be made again. In the last sentence, Huck is made to suggest a virtual identity between Miss Watson and Aunt Sally. But the two women are not at all alike. Aunt Sally is a sweet, motherly, entirely affectionate woman, from whom there is little need to escape because she has no aptitude for confinement. The only time she succeeds in confining Huck, she does so by *trusting* him. And so when the book says, "Aunt Sally she's going to adopt me and sivilize me and I can't stand it. I been there before," one can only conclude that it is not Huck talking about Aunt Sally, but Mark Twain talking, still, about the oppressive female piety of Miss Watson.

Something is badly awry here. At the end of this great book we are asked to believe—or to believe that Huck believes—that there are no choices between the "civilization" represented by pious slave owners like Miss Watson or lethal "gentlemen" like Colonel Sherburn and lighting out for the Territory. This hopeless polarity marks the exit of Mark Twain's highest imagination from his work. Afterwards we get *Pudd'nhead Wilson*, a fine book, but inferior to *Huckleberry Finn*, and then the inconsolable grief, bitterness, and despair of the last years.

It is arguable, I think, that our country's culture is still suspended as if at the end of *Huckleberry Finn*, assuming that its only choices are either a deadly "civilization" of piety and violence or an escape into some "Territory" where we may remain free of adulthood and community obligation. We want to be free; we want to have rights; we want to have power; we do not yet want much to do with responsibility. We have imagined the great and estimable freedom of boyhood, of which Huck Finn remains the finest spokesman. We have imagined the bachelorhoods of nature and genius and power: the contemplative, the artist, the hunter, the cowboy, the general, the president—lives dedicated and solitary in the Territory of individuality. But boyhood and bachelorhood have remained our norms of "liberation," for women as well as men. We have hardly begun to imagine the coming to responsibility that is the meaning, and the liberation, of growing up. We have hardly begun to imagine community life, and the tragedy that is at the heart of community life.

Mark Twain's avowed preference for boyhood, as the time of truthfulness, is well known. Beyond boyhood, he glimpsed the possibility of bachelorhood, an escape to "the Territory," where individual freedom and integrity might be maintained—and so, perhaps, he imagined Pudd'nhead Wilson, a solitary genius devoted to truth and justice, standing apart in the preserve of cynical honesty.

He also imagined Aunt Polly and Aunt Sally. They, I think, are the true grown-ups of the Mississippi novels. They have their faults, of course, which are the faults of their time and place, but mainly they are decent people, responsible members of the community, faithful to duties, capable of love, trust, and long-suffering, willing to care for orphan children. The characters of both women are affectionately drawn; Mark Twain evidently was moved by them. And yet he made no acknowledgment of their worth. He insists on regarding them as dampeners of youthful high spirits, and in the end he refuses to distinguish them at all from the objectionable Miss Watson.

There is, then, something stunted in *Huckleberry Finn*. I have hated to think so—for a long time I tried consciously *not* to think so—but it is so. What is stunted is the growth of Huck's character. When Mark Twain replaces Huck as author, he does so apparently to make sure that Huck remains a boy. Huck's growing up, which through the crisis of his fidelity to Jim ("All right, then, I'll *go* to hell") has been central to the drama of the book, is suddenly thwarted first by the Tom-foolery of Jim's "evasion" and then by Huck's planned escape to the "Territory." The real "evasion" of the last chapters is Huck's, or Mark Twain's, evasion of the community responsibility that would have been a natural and expectable next step after his declaration of loyalty to his friend. Mark Twain's failure or inability to imagine this possibility was a disaster for his finest character, Huck, whom we next see not as a grown man, but as partner in another boyish evasion, a fantastical balloon excursion to the Pyramids.

I am supposing, then, that *Huckleberry Finn* fails in failing to imagine a responsible, adult community life. And I am supposing further that this is the failure of Mark Twain's life, and of our life, so far, as a society.

Community life, as I suggested earlier, is tragic, and it is so because it involves unremittingly the need to survive mortality, partiality, and evil. Because Huck Finn and Mark Twain so clung to boyhood, and to the boy's vision of free bachelorhood, neither could enter community life as I am attempting to understand it. A boy can experience grief and horror, but he cannot experience that fulfillment and catharsis of grief, fear, and pity that we call tragedy and still remain a boy. Nor can he experience tragedy in solitude or as a stranger, for tragedy is experienceable only in the context of a beloved community. The fulfillment and catharsis that Aristotle described as the communal result of tragic drama is an artificial enactment of the way a mature community survives tragedy in fact. The community wisdom of tragic drama is in the implicit understanding that no community can survive that cannot survive the worst. Tragic drama attests to the community's need to survive the worst that it knows, or imagines, can happen.

In his own life, Mark Twain experienced deep grief over the deaths of loved ones, and also severe financial losses. But these experiences seem to have had the effect of isolating him, rather than binding him to a community. Great personal loss, moreover, is not much dealt with in those Mississippi books that are most native to his imagination: *Tom Sawyer*, *Huckleberry Finn*, and *Life on the Mississippi*. The only such event that I remember in those books is the story, in *Life on the Mississippi*, of his brother Henry's death after an explosion on the steamboat *Pennsylvania*. Twain's account of this is extremely moving, but it is peculiar in that he represents himself—though his mother, a brother, and a sister still lived—as Henry's *only* mourner. No other family member is mentioned.

What is wanting, apparently, is the tragic imagination that, through communal form or ceremony, permits great loss to be recognized, suffered, and borne, and that makes possible some sort of consolation and renewal. What is wanting is the return to the beloved community, or to the possibility of one. That would return us to a renewed and corrected awareness of our partiality and mortality, but also to healing and to joy in a renewed awareness of our love and hope for one another. Without that return we may know innocence and horror and grief, but not tragedy and joy, not consolation or forgiveness or redemption. There is grief and horror in Mark Twain's life and work, but not the tragic imagination or the imagined tragedy that finally delivers from grief and horror.

He seems instead to have gone deeper and deeper into grief and horror as his losses accumulated, and deeper into outrage as he continued to meditate on the injustices and cruelties of history. At the same time he withdrew further and further from community and the imagining of community, until at last his Hadleyburg—such a village as he had earlier written about critically enough, but with sympathy and good humor too—is used merely as a target. It receives an anonymous and indiscriminate retribution for its greed and self-righteousness—evils that community life has always had to oppose, correct, ignore, indulge, or forgive in order to survive. All observers of communities have been aware of such evils, Huck Finn having been one of the acutest of them, but now it is as if Huck has been replaced by Colonel Sherburn. "The Man that Corrupted Hadleyburg" is based on the devastating assumption that people are no better than their faults. In old age, Mark Twain had become obsessed with "the damned human race" and the malevolence of God—ideas that were severely isolating and, ultimately, self-indulgent. He was finally incapable of that magnanimity that is the most difficult and the most necessary: forgiveness of human nature and human circumstance. Given human nature and human circumstance, our only relief is in this forgiveness, which then restores us to community and its ancient cycle of loss and grief, hope and joy.

And so it seems to me that Mark Twain's example remains crucial for us, for both its virtues and its faults. He taught American writers to be writers by teaching them to be *regional* writers. The great gift of *Huckleberry Finn*, in itself and to us, is its ability to be regional without being provincial. The provincial is always self-conscious. It is the conscious sentimentalization of or condescension to or apology for a province, what I earlier called regionalism. At its most acute, it is the fear of provinciality. There is, as I said, none of that in the first thirty-two chapters of *Huckleberry Finn*. (In the final eleven chapters it is there in the person of Tom Sawyer, who is a self-made provincial.) Mark Twain apparently knew, or he had the grace to trust Huck to know, that *every* writer is a regional writer, even those who write about a fashionable region such as New York City. The value of this insight, embodied as it is in a great voice and a great tale, is simply unreckonable. If he had done nothing else, that would have made him indispensable to us.

But his faults are our own, just as much as his virtues. There are two chief faults and they are related: the yen to escape to the Territory, and retribution against the life that one has escaped or wishes to escape. Mark Twain was new, for his place, in his virtue. In his faults he was old, a spokesman for tendencies already long established in our history.

That these tendencies remain well established among us ought to be clear enough. Wallace Stegner had them in mind when he wrote in *The Sound of Mountain Water*:

> For many, the whole process of intellectual and literary growth is a movement, not through or beyond, but away from the people and society they know best, the faiths they still at bottom accept, the little raw provincial world for which they keep an apologetic affection.

Mr. Stegner's "away from" indicates, of course, an escape to the Territory—and there are many kinds of Territory to escape to. The Territory that hinterland writers have escaped to has almost always been first of all that of some metropolis or "center of culture." This is not inevitably dangerous; great cities are probably necessary to the life of the arts, and all of us who have gone to them have benefited. But once one has reached the city, other Territories open up, and some of these *are* dangerous. There is, first, the Territory of retribution against one's origins. In our country, this is not just a Territory, but virtually a literary genre. From the sophisticated, cosmopolitan city, one's old home begins to look like a "little raw provincial world." One begins to deplore "small town gossip" and "the suffocating proprieties of small town life"—forgetting that gossip occurs only among people who know one another and that propriety is a dead issue only among strangers. The danger is not just in the falsification, the false generalization, that necessarily attends a *distant* scorn or anger, but also in the loss of the subject or the vision of community life and in the very questionable exemption that scorners and avengers customarily issue to themselves.

And so there is the Territory of self-righteousness. It is easy to assume that we do not participate in what we are not in the presence of. But if we are members of a society, we participate, willynilly, in its evils. Not to know this is obviously to be in error, but it is also to neglect some of the most necessary and the most interesting work. How do we reduce our dependency on what is wrong? The answer to that question will necessarily be practical; the wrong will be correctable by practice and by practical standards. Another name for self-righteousness is economic and political unconsciousness.

There is also the Territory of historical self-righteousness: if *we* had lived south of the Ohio in 1830, *we* would not have owned slaves; if *we* had lived on the frontier, *we* would have killed no Indians, violated no treaties, stolen no land. The probability is overwhelming that if we had belonged to the generations we deplore, we too would have behaved deplorably. The probability is overwhelming that we *belong* to a generation that will be found by its successors to have behaved deplorably. Not to know that is, again, to be in error and to neglect essential work, and some of this work, as before, is work of the imagination. How can we imagine our situation or our history if we think we are superior to it?

Then there is the Territory of despair, where it is assumed that what is objectionable is "inevitable," and so again the essential work is neglected. How can we have something better if we do not imagine it? How can we imagine it if we do not hope for it? How can we hope for it if we do not attempt to realize it?

There is the Territory of the national or the global point of view, in which one does not pay attention to anything in particular.

Akin to that is the Territory of abstraction, a regionalism of the mind. This Territory originally belonged to philosophers, mathematicians, economists, tank thinkers, and the like, but now some claims are being staked out in it for literature. At a meeting in honor of *The Southern Review*, held in the fall of 1985 at Baton Rouge, one of the needs identified, according to an article in the *New York Times Book Review*,* was "to redefine Southernness without resort to geography." If the participants all agreed on any one thing, the article concluded,

> it is perhaps that accepted definitions of regionalism have been unnecessarily self-limiting up to now. The gradual disappearance of the traditional, material South does not mean that Southernness is disappearing, any more than blackness is threatened by integration, or sacredness by secularization. If anything, these metaregions . . . , based as they are upon values, achieve distinction in direct proportion to the homogenization of the physical world. By coming to terms with a concept of regionalism that is no longer based on geographical or material considerations, *The Southern Review* is sidestepping those forces that would organize the world around an unnatural consensus.

Parts of that statement are not comprehensible. Blackness, I would think, *would* be threatened by integration, and sacredness by secularization. Dilution, at least, is certainly implied in both instances. We might as well say that fire is a state of mind and thus is not threatened by water. And how might blackness and sacredness, which have never been regions, be "metaregions"? And is the natural world subject to limitless homogenization? There are, after all, southern species of plants and animals that will not thrive in the north, and vice versa.

This "metaregion," this region "without resort to geography," is a map without a territory, which is to say a map impossible to correct, a map subject to become fantastical and silly like that Southern chivalry-of-the-mind that Mark Twain so properly condemned. How this "metaregion" could resist homogenization and "unnatural consensus" is not clear. At any rate, it abandons the real region to the homogenizers: You just homogenize all you want to, and we will sit here being Southern in our minds.

* Mark K. Stengel, "Modernism on the Mississippi: The Southern Review 1935–85," *New York Times Book Review*, November 24, 1985, pp. 3, 35.

Similar to the Territory of abstraction is the Territory of artistic primacy or autonomy, in which it is assumed that no value is inherent in subjects but that value is conferred upon subjects by the art and the attention of the artist. The subjects of the world are only "raw material." As William Matthews writes in a recent article,* "A poet beginning to make something needs raw material, something to transform." For Marianne Moore, he says,

> subject matter is not in itself important, except that it gives her the opportunity to speak about something that engages her passions. What is important instead is what she can discover to say.

And he concludes:

> It is not, of course, the subject that is or isn't dull, but the quality of attention we do or do not pay to it, and the strength of our will to transform. Dull subjects are those we have failed.

This assumes that for the animals and humans who are not fine artists, who have discovered nothing to say, the world is dull, which is not true. It assumes also that attention is of interest in itself, which is not true either. In fact, attention is of value only insofar as it is paid in the proper discharge of an obligation. To pay attention is to come into the presence of a subject. In one of its root senses, it is to "stretch toward" a subject, in a kind of aspiration. We speak of "paying attention" because of a correct perception that attention is *owed*—that without our attention and our attending, our subjects, including ourselves, are endangered.

Mr. Matthews's trivializing of subjects in the interest of poetry industrializes the art. He is talking about an art oriented exclusively to production, like coal mining. Like an industrial entrepreneur, he regards the places and creatures and experiences of the world as "raw material," valueless until exploited.

The test of imagination, ultimately, is not the territory of art

*"Dull Subjects," *New England Review and Bread Loaf Quarterly*, Winter 1985, pp. 142–152.

or the territory of the mind, but the territory underfoot. That is not to say that there is no territory of art or of the mind, only that it is not a separate territory. It is not exempt either from the principles above it or from the country below it. It is a territory, then, that is subject to correction—by, among other things, paying attention. To remove it from the possibility of correction is finally to destroy art and thought, and the territory underfoot as well.

Memory, for instance, must be a pattern upon the actual country, not a cluster of relics in a museum or a written history. What Barry Lopez speaks of as a sort of invisible landscape of communal association and usage must serve the visible as a guide and as a protector; the visible landscape must verify and correct the invisible. Alone, the invisible landscape becomes false, sentimental, and useless, just as the visible landscape, alone, becomes a strange land, threatening to humans and vulnerable to human abuse.

To assume that the context of literature is "the literary world" is, I believe, simply wrong. That its real habitat is the household and the community—that it can and does affect, even in practical ways, the life of a place—may not be recognized by most theorists and critics for a while yet. But they will finally come to it, because finally they will have to. And when they do, they will renew the study of literature and restore it to importance.

Emerson in "The American Scholar," worrying about the increasing specialization of human enterprises, thought that the individual, to be whole, "must sometimes return from his own labor to embrace all the other laborers"—a solution that he acknowledged to be impossible. The result, he saw, was that "man is thus metamorphosed into a thing, into many things." The solution that he apparently did think possible was a return out of specialization and separateness to the human definition, so that a thinker or scholar would not be a "mere thinker," a thinking specialist, but "Man Thinking." But this return is not meant to be a retreat into abstraction, for Emerson understood "Man Thinking" as a thinker committed to action: "Action is with the scholar subordinate, but it is essential. Without it, he is not yet man."

And action, of course, implies place and community. There can be disembodied thought, but not disembodied action. Action—embodied thought—requires local and communal reference. To act, in short, is to live. Living "is a total act. Thinking is a partial act." And one does not live alone. Living is a communal act, whether or not its communality is acknowledged. And so Emerson writes:

> I grasp the hands of those next me, and take my place in the ring to suffer and to work, taught by an instinct, that so shall the dumb abyss be vocal with speech.

Emerson's spiritual heroism can sometimes be questionable or tiresome, but he can also write splendidly accurate, exacting sentences, and that is one of them. We see how it legislates against what we now call "groupiness." Neighborhood is a given condition, not a contrived one; he is not talking about a "planned community" or a "network," but about the necessary interdependence of those who are "next" each other. We see how it invokes dance, acting in concert, as a metaphor of almost limitless reference. We see how the phrase "to suffer and to work" refuses sentimentalization. We see how common work, common suffering, and a common willingness to join and belong are understood as the conditions that make speech possible in "the dumb abyss" in which we are divided.

This leads us, probably, to as good a definition of the beloved community as we can hope for: common experience and common effort on a common ground to which one willingly belongs. The life of such a community has been very little regarded in American literature. Our writers have been much more concerned with the individual who is misunderstood or mistreated by a community that is in no sense beloved, as in *The Scarlet Letter*. From Thoreau to Hemingway and his successors, a great deal of sympathy and interest has been given to the individual as pariah or gadfly or exile. In Faulkner, a community is the subject, but it is a community disintegrating, as it was doomed to do by the original sins of land greed, violent honor, and slavery. There are in Faulkner some characters who keep alive the hope of community, or at least the fundamental decencies on which community depends, and in Faulkner, as in Mark Twain, these are chiefly women: Dilsey, Lena Grove, the properly outraged Mrs. Littlejohn.

The one American book I know that is about a beloved community—a settled, established white American community with a sustaining common culture, and mostly beneficent toward both its members and its place—is Sarah Orne Jewett's *The Country of the Pointed Firs*. The community that the book describes, the coastal village of Dunnet, Maine, and the neighboring islands and back country, is an endangered species on the book's own evidence: many of its characters are old and childless, without heirs or successors—and with the Twentieth Century ahead of it, it could not last. But though we see it in its last days, we see it whole.

We see it whole, I think, because we see it both in its time and in its timelessness. The centerpiece of the book, the Bowden family reunion, is described in the particularity of a present act, but it is perceived also—as such an event must be—as a reenactment; to see is to remember:

> There was a wide path mowed for us across the field, and, as we moved along, the birds flew up out of the thick second crop of clover, and the bees hummed as if it still were June. There was a flashing of white gulls over the water where the fleet of boats rode the low waves together in the cove, swaying their small masts as if they kept time to our steps. The plash of the water could be heard faintly, yet still be heard; we might have been a company of ancient Greeks.

Thus, though it precisely renders its place and time, the book never subsides into the flimsy contemporaneity of "local color." The narrator of the book is one who departs and returns, and her returns are homecomings—to herself as well as to the place:

The first salt wind from the east, the first sight of a lighthouse set boldly on its outer rock, the flash of a gull, the waiting procession of seaward-bound firs on an island, made me feel solid and definite again, instead of a poor incoherent being. Life was resumed, and anxious living blew away as if it had not been. I could not breathe deep enough or long enough. It was a return to happiness.

Anyone acquainted with the sentimentalities of American regionalism will look on that word "happiness" with suspicion. But here it is not sentimental, for the work and suffering of the community are fully faced and acknowledged. The narrator's return is not to an idyll of the boondocks; it is a re-entrance into Emerson's "ring." The community is happy in that it has survived its remembered tragedies, has re-shaped itself coherently around its known losses, has included kindly its eccentrics, invalids, oddities, and even its one would-be exile. The wonderful heroine of the book, and its emblem, Mrs. Elmira Todd, a childless widow, who in her youth "had loved one who was far above her," is a healer—a grower, gatherer, and dispenser of medicinal herbs.

She is also a dispenser of intelligent talk about her kinfolk and neighbors. More than any book I know, this one makes its way by conversation, engrossing exchanges of talk in which Mrs. Todd and many others reveal to the narrator their life and history and geography. And perhaps the great cultural insight of the book is stated by Mrs. Todd:

> Conversation's got to have some root in the past, or else you've got to explain every remark you make, an' it wears a person out.

The conversation wells up out of memory, and in a sense *is* the community, the presence of its past and its hope, speaking in the dumb abyss.

1987

THE RESPONSIBILITY
OF THE POET

To speak of the qualities of literary works is risky, of course. But one speaks, even so, believing that one is right and aware that, after all, there is only one other possibility.

To speak of "the responsibility of the poet," on the other hand, one must reconcile oneself both to the possibility of being, at best, no more than partly right and to the certainty of multifarious and passionate disagreement. Such an exercise is justifiable only on the ground that one would like to be a responsible poet, and that one cannot hope to be without thinking the matter over.

It has seemed to me increasingly that a poem—a good poem —exists at the center of a complex reminding, to which it relates as both cause and effect. The process of this reminding is too complex ever to be fully mapped or explained, and therefore the order of the following remarks about it is somewhat arbitrary.

Fundamentally, the existence of a poem reminds first its poet and then its readers of the technical means of poetry, which is to say its power as speech or song: the play of line against syntax and against stanza; the play of variation against form and against theme; the play of phrase against line, and of phrase against phrase within the line; the play of likenesses and differences of sounds; the play of statement with and against music; the play of rhyme against rhythm and as rhythm; the play of the poem as a made thing with and within and against the histories—personal and literary, national and local—that produce it.

A poem, that is, has the power to remind poet and reader alike of things they have read and heard. Also—and this is partly why the subject is so complex—it has the power to remind them of things that they have not read and heard, but that have been read and heard by others whom they *have* read and heard.

Thus the art, so private in execution, is also communal and filial. It can only exist as a common ground between the poet and other poets and other people, living and dead. Any poem worth the name is the product of a convocation. It exists, literally, by recalling past voices into presence. This has been no more memorably stated than in Spenser's apostrophe to Chaucer in Book 4 of *The Faerie Queene*:

> through infusion sweet
> Of thine own spirit, which doth in me survive,
> I follow here the footing of thy feet.

Poetry can be written only because it has been written. As a new poem is made, not only with the art but within it, past voices are convoked—to be changed, little or much, by the addition of another voice.

A poem, too, may remind poet and reader alike of what is remembered or ought to be remembered—as in elegies, poems of history, love poems, celebrations of nature, poems of praise or worship, or poems as prayers. One of the functions of the music or formality of poetry is to make memorable. Even the rhyme beginning "Thirty days hath September" has the dignity of indispensability.

By its formal integrity a poem reminds us of the formal integrity of other works, creatures, and structures of the world. The form of a good poem is, in a way perhaps not altogether explainable or demonstrable, an analogue of the forms of other things. By its form it alludes to other forms, evokes them, resonates with them, and so becomes a part of the system of analogies or harmonies by which we live. Thus the poet affirms and collaborates in the formality of the Creation. This, I think, is a matter of supreme, and mostly unacknowledged, importance.

A poem reminds us also of the spiritual elation that we call "inspiration" or "gift." Or perhaps we ought to say that it should do so, it should be humble enough to do so, because we know that no permanently valuable poem is made by the merely intentional manipulation of its scrutable components. Hence, it reminds us of love. It is amateur work, lover's work. What we now call "professionalism" is anathema to it. A good poem reminds us of love because it cannot be written or read in distraction; it cannot be written or understood by anyone thinking of praise or publication or promotion. It is ruined utterly by what Donald Davie has called "the fluctuations of philistine but sophisticated fashion."

We are now inclined to make much of this distinction between amateur and professional, but it is reassuring to know that these words first were used in opposition to each other less than two hundred years ago. Before the first decade of the nineteenth century, no one felt the need for such a distinction—which established itself, I suppose, because of the industrial need to separate love from work, and so it was made at first to discriminate in favor of professionalism. To those who wish to defend the possibility of good or responsible work, it remains useful today because of the need to discriminate *against* professionalism.

Professional standards, the standards of ambition and selfishness, are always sliding downward toward expense, ostentation, and mediocrity. They tend always to narrow the ground of judgment. But amateur standards, the standards of love, are always straining upward toward the humble and the best. They enlarge the ground of judgment. The context of love is the world.

The standards of love are inseparable from the process or system of reminding that I am talking about. This reminding, I think, must be our subject if we want to understand the responsibility of the poet; it is to a considerable extent what poets respond to, and is to a considerable extent what they respond with.

This process, as I said, probably cannot be fully explained, but sometimes it is partly explainable, and what can be explained may be suggestive of what cannot be. For example, I can partly explain the reminding that is the source, or maybe we could say the location, of Donald Davie's poem "Advent." This poem has been important to me since I first read it in the Vanderbilt literary magazine several years ago. I have been back to it many times, first of all because I like and admire it and it is necessary to me; I have tried, on all my returns to it, to make sure that I have heard it correctly and understood it exactly. But I have returned to it also because of its relation to the modern issue of originality.

Is the poem original? As the times and lore of modern poetry have defined the term, I don't think it is. It is about spiritual distraction or restlessness, which it sets forth as a problem in six of its seven stanzas and then resolves in the seventh:

> Self-contradictions, I
> Have heard, do not bewilder
> That providential care.
> Switch and reverse as he
> Will, this one I know,
> One whose need meets his
> Prevents him everywhere.

The first six stanzas employ a manner of language that we recognize from Mr. Davie's essays: a considering, painstaking language, troubling toward the justice of exactitude. And then suddenly this burden is borne lightly as the poem resolves thematically and musically in the last stanza. This, on the face of it, can be identified as competence of a high order. It is masterful work. But the poem makes no spectacular technical innovation, and, heaven knows, there is nothing new in its "message."

The poem nevertheless originates authentic feeling; it claims attention and respect. To account for this, it is necessary to place the poem within its pattern of reminding, which we may as well say is the Judeo-Christian tradition as it begins in the Bible and threads its way through our culture and literature. One can hardly read this poem without being reminded of the story of Jonah, of the parable of the prodigal son, of George Herbert's

"The Collar." One may be reminded, too, of certain prosodic resolutions in the poems of Herbert, and of the tawdriness of spiritual irresolution in the work of T. S. Eliot. And of course one is reminded of sermons. The theme of this poem has been stated and re-stated in thousands of sermons that were spoken in the sleep of both speakers and hearers, spoken in the very sleep of the language. But this poem claims our attention and respect—claims our respect and *therefore* our attention—and thus rises up through that sleep. How does it do so? It does so, I think, by its justness and its music. By its justness and its music it charges its language with meaning; it adds itself authentically to its pattern of reminding, and thus re-awakens it and makes it new. It is original, then, not in somehow escaping its history, but in causing its history to resound and sing around it.

1988

Part III

GOD AND COUNTRY

The subject of Christianity and ecology is endlessly, perhaps infinitely, fascinating. It is fascinating theologically and artistically because of our never-to-be-satisfied curiosity about the relation between a made thing and its maker. It is fascinating practically because we are unrelentingly required to honor in all things the relation between the world and its Maker, and because that requirement implies another, equally unrelenting, that we ourselves, as makers, should always honor that greater making; we are required, that is, to study the ways of working well, and those ways are endlessly fascinating. The subject of Christianity and ecology also is politically fascinating, to those of us who are devoted both to biblical tradition and to the defense of the earth, because we are always hankering for the support of the churches, which seems to us to belong, properly and logically, to our cause.

This latter fascination, though not the most difficult and fearful, is certainly the most frustrating, for the fact simply is that the churches, which claim to honor God as the "maker of heaven and earth," have lately shown little inclination to honor the earth or to protect it from those who would dishonor it.

Organized Christianity seems, in general, to have made peace with "the economy" by divorcing itself from economic issues, and this, I think, has proved to be a disaster, both religious and economic. The reason for this, on the side of religion, is suggested by the adjective "organized." It is clearly possible that, in the condition of the world as the world now is, organization can force upon an institution a character that is alien or even antithetical to it. The *organized* church comes immediately under a compulsion to think of itself, and identify itself to the world, not as an institution synonymous with its truth and its membership, but as a hodgepodge of funds, properties, projects, and offices, all urgently requiring economic support. The organized church makes peace with a destructive economy and divorces itself from economic issues because it is economically compelled to do so. Like any other public institution so organized, the organized church is dependent on "the economy"; it cannot survive apart from those economic practices that its truth forbids and that its vocation is to correct. If it comes to a choice between the extermination of the fowls of the air and the lilies of the field and the extermination of a building fund, the organized church will elect—indeed, has already elected—to save the building fund. The irony is compounded and made harder to bear by the fact that the building fund can be preserved by crude applications of money, but the fowls of the air and the lilies of the field can be preserved only by true religion, by the *practice* of a proper love and respect for them as the creatures of God. No wonder so many sermons are devoted exclusively to "spiritual" subjects. If one is living by the tithes of history's most destructive economy, then the disembodiment of the soul becomes the chief of worldly conveniences.

There are many manifestations of this tacit alliance between the organized churches and "the economy," but I need to speak only of two in order to make my point. The first is the phrase "full-time Christian service," which the churches of my experience have used exclusively to refer to the ministry, thereby at once making of the devoted life a religious specialty or career and removing the possibility of devotion from other callings. Thus the $50,000-a-year preacher is a "full-time Christian servant," whereas a $20,000- or a $10,000-a-year farmer, or a farmer going broke, so far as the religious specialists are concerned, must serve "the economy" in his work or in his failure and serve God in his spare time. The professional class is likewise free to serve itself in its work and to serve God by giving the church its ten percent. The churches in this way excerpt sanctity from the human economy and its work just as Cartesian science has ex-

>

cerpted it from the material creation. And it is easy to see the interdependence of these two desecrations: the desecration of nature would have been impossible without the desecration of work, and vice versa.

The second manifestation I want to speak of is the practice, again common in the churches of my experience, of using the rural ministry as a training ground for young ministers and as a means of subsidizing their education. No church official, apparently, sees any logical, much less any spiritual, problem in sending young people to minister to country churches before they have, according to their institutional superiors, become eligible to be ministers. These student ministers invariably leave the rural congregations that have sponsored or endured their educations as soon as possible once they have their diplomas in hand. The denominational hierarchies, then, evidently regard country places in exactly the same way as "the economy" does: as sources of economic power to be exploited for the advantage of "better" places. The country people will be used to educate ministers for the benefit of city people (in wealthier churches) who, obviously, are thought more deserving of educated ministers. This, I am well aware, is mainly the fault of the church organizations; it is not a charge that can be made to stick to any young minister in particular: not all ministers should be country ministers, just as not all people should be country people. And yet it is a fact that in the more than fifty years that I have known my own rural community, many student ministers have been "called" to serve in its churches, but not one has ever been "called" to stay. The message that country people get from their churches, then, is the same message that they get from "the economy": that, as country people, they do not matter much and do not deserve much consideration. And this inescapably imposes an economic valuation on spiritual things. According to the modern church, as one of my Christian friends said to me, "The soul of the plowboy ain't worth as much as the soul of the delivery boy."

If the churches are mostly indifferent to the work and the

people by which the link between economy and ecosystem must be enacted, it is no wonder that they are mostly indifferent to the fate of the ecosystems themselves. One must ask, then: is this state of affairs caused by Christian truth or by the failures and errors of Christian practice? My answer is that it is caused by the failures and errors of Christian practice. The evident ability of most church leaders to be "born again in Christ" without in the least discomforting their faith in the industrial economy's bill of goods, however convenient and understandable it may be, is not scriptural.

Anyone making such a statement must deal immediately with the belief of many non-Christian environmentalists as well as at least some Christians that Genesis 1:28, in which God instructs Adam and Eve to "be fruitful and multiply and replenish the earth, and subdue it," gives unconditional permission to human-kind to use the world as it pleases. Such a reading of Genesis 1:28 is contradicted by virtually all the rest of the Bible, as many people by now have pointed out. The ecological teaching of the Bible is simply inescapable: God made the world because He wanted it made. He thinks the world is good, and He loves it. It is His world; He has never relinquished title to it. And He has never revoked the conditions, bearing on His gift to us of the use of it, that oblige us to take excellent care of it. If God loves the world, then how might any person of faith be excused for not loving it or justified in destroying it?

But of course, those who see in Genesis 1:28 the source of all our abuse of the natural world (most of them apparently having read no more of the Bible than that verse) are guilty of an extremely unintelligent misreading of Genesis 1:28 itself. How, for example, would one arrange to "replenish the earth" if "subdue" means, as alleged, "conquer" or "defeat" or "destroy"?

We have in fact in the biblical tradition, rooted in the Bible but amplified in agrarian, literary, and other cultural traditions stemming from the Bible, the idea of stewardship as conditioned by the idea of usufruct. George Perkins Marsh was invoking biblical tradition when he wrote, in 1864, that "man has too long forgotten that the earth was given to him for usufruct alone, not for consumption, still less for profligate waste." The Mormon essayist Hugh Nibley invoked it explicitly when he wrote that "man's dominion is a call to service, not a license to exterminate."

That service, stewardship, is the responsible care of property belonging to another. And by this the Bible does not mean an absentee landlord, but one living on the property, profoundly and intimately involved in its being and its health, as Elihu says to Job: "if he gather unto himself his spirit and his breath; All flesh shall perish together." All creatures live by God's spirit, portioned out to them, and breathe His breath. To "lay up . . . treasures in heaven," then, cannot mean to be spiritual at the earth's expense, or to despise or condemn the earth for the sake of heaven. It means exactly the opposite: do not desecrate or depreciate these gifts, which take part with us in the being of God, by turning them into worldly "treasure"; do not reduce life to money or to any other mere quantity.

The idea of usufruct gives this point to the idea of stewardship, and makes it practical and economic. Usufruct, the *Oxford English Dictionary* says, is "the right of temporary possession, use, or enjoyment of the advantages of property belonging to another, so far as may be had without causing damage or prejudice to this." It is hardly a "free-market economy" that the Bible prescribes. Large accumulations of land were, and are, forbidden because the dispossession and privation of some cannot be an acceptable or normal result of the economic activity of others, for that destroys a people as a people; it destroys the community. Usury was, and is, forbidden because the dispossession and privation of some should not be regarded by others as an economic opportunity, for that is contrary to neighborliness; it destroys the community. And the greed that destroys the community also destroys the land. What the Bible proposes is a moral economy, the standard of which is the health of properties belonging to God.

But we have considered so far only those things of the Creation that can be included within the human economy—the usable properties, so to speak. What about the things that are outside the human economy? What about the things that from the point of view of human need are useless or only partly usable? What about the places that, as is increasingly evident, we should not use at all? Obviously we must go further, and the Bible can take us further. Many passages take us beyond a merely economic stewardship, but the one that has come to seem most valuable to me is Revelation 4:11, because I think it proposes an indispensable standard for the stewardship both of things in use and of useless things and things set aside from use: "Thou art worthy, O Lord, to receive glory and honour and power: for thou hast created all things, and for thy pleasure they are and were created."

The implications of this verse are relentlessly practical. The ideas that we are permitted to use things that are pleasing to God, that we have nothing at all to use that is not pleasing to Him, and that necessarily implicated in the power to use is the power to misuse and destroy are troubling, and indeed frightening, ideas. But they are consoling, too, precisely insofar as we have the ability to use well and the goodness or the character required to limit use or to forbear to use.

Our responsibility, then, as stewards, the responsibility that inescapably goes with our dominion over the other creatures, according to Revelation 4:11, is to safeguard God's pleasure in His work. And we can do that, I think (I don't know how else we could do it), by safeguarding *our* pleasure in His work, and our pleasure in our own work. Or, if we no longer can trust ourselves to be more than economic machines, then we must do it by safeguarding the pleasure of children in God's work and in ours. It is impossible, admittedly, to give an accurate economic value to the goodness of good work, much less to the goodness of an unspoiled forest or prairie or desert, or to the goodness of pure sunlight or water or air. And yet we are required to make an economy that honors such goods and is conversant with them. An economy that ignores them, as our present one does, "builds a Hell in Heaven's despite."

As a measure of how far we have "progressed" in our industrial economy, let me quote a part of a sentence from the prayer "For Every Man in His Work" from the 1928 *Book of Common Prayer*: "Deliver us, we beseech thee, in our several callings, from the service of mammon, that we may do the work which thou givest us to do, in truth, in beauty, and in righteousness, with singleness of heart as thy servants, and to the benefit of our fellow men." What is astonishing about that prayer is that it is a relic. Throughout the history of the industrial revolution, it has become steadily less prayable. The industrial nations are now divided, almost entirely, into a professional or executive class that has not the least intention of working in truth, beauty, and righteousness, as God's servants, or to the benefit of their fellow men, and an underclass that has no choice in the matter. Truth, beauty, and righteousness now have, and can have, nothing to do with the economic life of most people. This alone, I think, is sufficient to account for the orientation of most churches to religious feeling, increasingly feckless, as opposed to religious thought or religious behavior.

I acknowledge that I feel deeply estranged from most of the manifestations of organized religion, partly for reasons that I have mentioned. Yet I am far from thinking that one can somehow become righteous by carrying protestantism to the logical conclusion of a one-person church. We all belong, at least, to the problem. "There is . . . a price to be paid," Philip Sherrard says, "for fabricating around us a society which is as artificial and as mechanized as our own, and this is that we can exist in it only on condition that we adapt ourselves to it. This is our punishment."*

We all, obviously, are to some extent guilty of this damnable adaptation. We all are undergoing this punishment. But as Philip Sherrard well knows, it is a punishment that we can set our hearts against, an adaptation that we can try with all our might to undo. We can ally ourselves with those things that are worthy: light, air, water, earth; plants and animals; human families and communities; the traditions of decent life, good work, and responsible thought; the religious traditions; the essential stories and songs.

It is presumptuous, personally and historically, to assume that one is a part of a "saving remnant." One had better doubt that one deserves such a distinction, and had better understand that there may, after all, be nothing left to save. Even so, if one wishes to save anything not protected by the present economy—topsoil, groves of old trees, the possibility of the goodness or health of anything, even the economic relevance of the biblical tradition—one is a part of a remnant, and a dwindling remnant too, though not without hope, and not without the necessary instructions, the most pertinent of which, perhaps, is this, also from Revelation: "Be watchful, and strengthen the things which remain, that are ready to die."

1988

---

* *The Rape of Man and Nature*, Golgonooza Press (England), pp. 71–72.

A PRACTICAL HARMONY

In 1913, seventy-five years ago, Liberty Hyde Bailey retired from his post at Cornell after a quarter-century during which he had been, first, Professor of Horticulture, and then Director and Dean of the New York State College of Agriculture and Director of the Experiment Station. Two years later he published a little book with the remarkable title *The Holy Earth*. In it he wrote: "Most of our difficulty with the earth lies in the effort to do what perhaps ought not to be done. . . . A good part of agriculture is to learn how to adapt one's work to nature. . . . To live in right relation with his natural conditions is one of the first lessons that a wise farmer or any other wise man learns."*

Was that perhaps the exhalation of a restless soul, having cast off at last its academic bonds? No, it was not. For in 1905, the second year of his deanship, he had published a book entitled *The Outlook to Nature*, in which he spoke of nature as "the norm." "If nature is the norm," he wrote, "then the necessity for correcting and amending the abuses of civilization becomes baldly apparent by very contrast." And he added, "The return to nature affords the very means of acquiring the incentive and energy for ambitious and constructive work of a high order."†

Dean Bailey was not, of course, against the necessary pursuits of the human economy. He was merely for bringing those pursuits into harmony with nature, which he understood as their source and pattern. I mention him here not just because he is one of the inevitable measures of the subsequent history of the Land Grant system, but because, as an officer of that system, he spoke

* *The Holy Earth*, reprinted by The Christian Rural Fellowship, 1946, p. 9.
† *The Outlook to Nature*, Macmillan, 1905, p. 8.

for a view of things that, however threatened in his time and since, goes back to the roots of our experience as human beings.

This view of things holds that we can live only in and from nature, and that we have, therefore, an inescapable obligation to be nature's students and stewards and to live in harmony with her. This is a theme of both the classical and the biblical traditions. It is not so prominent a theme as we could wish, perhaps because until lately it was taken for granted, but it is a constant theme, and it is more prominent than modern education prepares us to expect. Virgil, for example, states it boldly at the beginning of *The Georgics*, written between 36 and 29 B.C.:

> . . . before we plow an unfamiliar patch
> It is well to be informed about the winds,
> About the variations in the sky,
> The native traits and habits of the place,
> What each locale permits, and what denies.*

And several hundred years before that Job, the man of Uz, had said to his visitors:

> . . . ask now the beasts, and they shall teach thee; and the fowls of
> the air, and they shall tell thee:
> Or speak to the earth, and it shall teach thee: and the fishes of the
> sea shall declare unto thee.

In the English poetic tradition this theme is restated by voice after voice. Edmund Spenser, toward the end of the sixteenth century, described Nature as "the equall mother" of all creatures, who "knittest each to each, as brother unto brother." For that reason, perhaps, he sees her also as the instructor of creatures and the ultimate earthly judge of their behavior.

The theme was stated again by Shakespeare in *As You Like It*, in which the forest performs the role of teacher and judge, a role that is explicitly acknowledged by Touchstone: "You have said;

*Translation by Smith Palmer Bovie, The University of Chicago Press, 1966, p. 5.

but whether wisely or no, let the forest judge." And Milton stated
the theme, again forthrightly, in *Comus*, when the Lady says of
Nature:

> she, good cateress,
> Means her provision only to the good
> That live according to her sober laws
> And holy dictate of spare Temperance.

And Alexander Pope stated it, as plainly as the others, in his *Epistle to Burlington*, in which he counseled gardeners to "let Nature
never be forgot" and to "Consult the Genius of the Place in all."

After Pope, so far as I know, this theme departs from English
poetry. Later poets were inclined to see nature and humankind as
radically divided and were no longer much interested in the issues of a *practical* harmony between the land and its human inhabitants. The romantic poets, who subscribed to the modern
doctrine of the preeminence of the human mind, tended to look
upon nature not as anything they might ever have practical dealings with, but as a reservoir of symbols.

The theme of nature as instructor and judge seems to have
been taken up next by a series of agricultural writers in our own
century. I say "series" rather than "succession" because I don't
know to what extent these people have worked consciously under the influence of predecessors. I suspect that the succession, in
both poetry and agriculture, may lie in the familial and communal handing down of the agrarian common culture, rather
than in any succession of teachers and students in the literary culture or in the schools. I do not, for example, know the ancestry of
the mind of Liberty Hyde Bailey, though I would guess with some
confidence that he is one of the heirs of Thomas Jefferson. Jefferson's preoccupation with what he called "horizontal plowing"
and other issues of proper husbandry was certainly an attempt of
a "wise farmer" to farm "in right relation to his natural conditions." But such a coincidence of thoughts does not establish
succession. There remains the possibility—and I think it is a

strong one—that, though Bailey undoubtedly knew the example of Jefferson, both men worked out of predisposing ideas and assumptions handed down to them as children.

One of Liberty Hyde Bailey's contemporaries was J. Russell Smith, whose interests and loyalties as an academician will seem as improbable to us as those of Dean Bailey. In 1929, when he was professor of economic geography at Columbia University, J. Russell Smith published a book entitled *Tree Crops*, the aims of which were at once ecological and patriotic. The book, he said, was "written to persons of imagination who love trees and love their country." His concern was the destruction of the hill lands by agriculture: "Man has carried to the hills the agriculture of the flat plain." Smith's answer to this problem was that "*farming should fit the land*." "Trees," he wrote, "are the natural crop plants for all such places." The great virtue of trees is that they are perennials; a hillside planted in trees would be "a permanent institution." Tree crops, he believed, could restore both the ecological and the human health of the hilly land. His vision was this:

> I see a million hills green with crop-yielding trees and a million neat farm homes snuggled in the hills. These beautiful tree farms hold the hills from Boston to Austin, from Atlanta to Des Moines. The hills of my vision have farming that fits them and replaces the poor pasture, the gullies, and the abandoned lands that characterize today so large a part of these hills.

That J. Russell Smith was aware of the early work of Albert Howard we know from a footnote in *Tree Crops*. Whether or not Howard knew Smith's work, I do not know. Nevertheless, when Sir Albert Howard (as he came to be) published *An Agricultural Testament* in 1940, his message was essentially the same as Smith's (and essentially the same as that of the Book of Job, Virgil, Spenser, Shakespeare, Milton, Pope, and Liberty Hyde Bailey). Nature, he said, is "the supreme farmer." If one wants to know how to farm well, one must study the forest. In a paragraph as allegorical as *The Faerie Queene*, he wrote:

The main characteristic of Nature's farming can therefore be summed up in a few words. Mother earth never attempts to farm without live stock; she always raises mixed crops; great pains are taken to preserve the soil and to prevent erosion; the mixed vegetable and animal wastes are converted into humus; there is no waste; the processes of growth and the processes of decay balance one another; ample provision is made to maintain large reserves of fertility; the greatest care is taken to store the rainfall; both plants and animals are left to protect themselves against disease.

Sir Albert Howard mentioned the prairie on the same page with the passage I just quoted, but he was native to country that was by nature forest land. It remained for Wes and Dana Jackson and their fellow workers at the Land Institute to take the logical next step to the proposition that if one lives on the prairie, one must learn to farm by studying the prairie. The difference between the native prairie and the modern grainfield is a critical one, and it provides the only feasible basis for criticism and correction of the grainfield. The principle is stated by Wes in Chapter 8 of *New Roots for Agriculture*: "The agricultural human's pull historically has been toward the monoculture of annuals. Nature's pull is toward a polyculture of perennials."

If the work of the Land Institute is innovative, it is so partly in response to a long tradition and an old hope. It is not merely another episode in our time's random pursuit of novelty. The Institute's purpose, as set forth by Wes Jackson and Marty Bender in their article "Investigations into Perennial Polyculture," is at once new and recognizably ancient: "We believe that the best agriculture for any region is the one that best mimics the region's natural ecosystems. . . . Our goal is . . . to create prairielike grain fields."

The goal is a harmony between the human economy and nature that will preserve both nature and humanity, and this is a traditional goal. The world is now divided between those who adhere to this ancient purpose and those who by intention do not—

a division that is of far more portent for the future of the world than any of the presently recognized national or political or economic divisions.

The remarkable thing about this division is its relative newness. The idea that we should obey nature's laws and live harmoniously with her as good husbanders and stewards of her gifts is old. And I believe that until fairly recently our destructions of nature were more or less unwitting—the by-products, so to speak, of our ignorance or weakness or depravity. It is our present principled and elaborately rationalized rape and plunder of the natural world that is a new thing under the sun.

1988

AN ARGUMENT

FOR DIVERSITY

*Elegant solutions will be predicated upon
the uniqueness of place.*   JOHN TODD

I live in and have known all my life the northern corner of Henry
County, Kentucky. The country here is narrowly creased and
folded; it is a varied landscape whose main features are these:

1. A rolling upland of which some of the soil is good and
some, because of abuse, is less so. This upland is well suited to
mixed farming, which was, in fact, traditional to it, but which is
less diversified now than it was a generation ago. Some row-
cropping is possible here, but even the best-lying ridges are vulnerable to erosion and probably not more than ten percent
should be broken in any year. It is a kind of land that needs grass
and grazing animals, and it is excellent for this use.

2. Wooded bluffs where the upland breaks over into the valleys of the creeks and the Kentucky River. Along with virtually all
of this region, most of these bluffs have been cleared and cropped
at one time or another. They should never have been cropped,
and because of their extreme vulnerability to erosion they should
be logged only with the greatest skill and care. These bluffs are
now generally forested, though not many old-growth stands remain.

3. Slopes of gentler declivity below the bluffs and elsewhere.
Some of these slopes are grassed and, with close care, are main-
tainable as pasture. Until World War II they were periodically
cropped, in a version of slash-and-burn agriculture that resulted

in serious damage by erosion. Now much of this land is covered with trees thirty or forty years old.

4. Finally, there are the creek and river bottoms, some of which are subject to flooding. Much of this land is suitable for intensive row-cropping, which, under the regime of industrial agriculture, has sometimes been too intensive.

Within these four general divisions this country is extremely diverse. To familiarity and experience, the landscape divides into many small facets or aspects differentiated by the kind or quality of soil and by slope, exposure, drainage, rockiness, and so on. In the two centuries during which European races have occupied this part of the country, the best of the land has sometimes been well used, under the influence of good times and good intentions. But virtually none of it has escaped ill use under the influence of bad times or ignorance, need or greed. Some of it—the steeper, more marginal areas—never has been well used. Of virtually all this land it may be said that the national economy has prescribed ways of use but not ways of care. It is now impossible to imagine any immediate way that most of this land might receive excellent care. The economy, as it now is, prescribes plunder of the landowners and abuse of the land.

The connection of the American economy to this place—in comparison, say, to the connection of the American economy to just about any university—has been unregarding and ungenerous. Indeed, the connection has been almost entirely exploitive—and it has never been more exploitive than it is now. Increasingly, from the beginning, most of the money made on the products of this place has been made in other places. Increasingly the ablest young people of this place have gone away to receive a college education, which has given them a "professional status" too often understood as a license to become the predators of such places as this one that they came from. The destruction of the human community, the local economy, and the natural health of such a place as this is now looked upon not as a "trade-off," a possibly regrettable "price of progress," but as a good, virtually a national goal.

Recently I heard, on an early-morning radio program, a university economist explaining the benefits of off-farm work for farm women: that these women are increasingly employed off the farm, she said, has made them "full partners" in the farm's economy. Never mind that this is a symptom of economic desperation and great unhappiness on the farm. And never mind the value, which was more than economic, of these women's previous contribution *on* the farm to the farm family's life and economy—in what was, many of them would have said, a full partnership. *Now* they are "earning forty-five percent of total family income"; *now* they are playing "a major role." The forty-five percent and the "major role" are allowed to defray all other costs. That the farm family now furnishes labor and (by its increased consumption) income to the economy that is destroying it is seen simply as an improvement. Thus the abstract and extremely tentative value of money is thoughtlessly allowed to replace the particular and fundamental values of the lives of household and community. Obviously, we need to stop thinking about the economic functions of individuals for a while, and try to learn to think of the economic functions of communities and households. We need to try to understand the long-term economies of places—places, that is, that are considered as dwelling places for humans and their fellow creatures, not as exploitable resources.

What happens when farm people take up "off-farm work"? The immediate result is that they must be replaced by chemicals and machines and other purchases from an economy adverse and antipathetic to farming, which means that the remaining farmers are put under yet greater economic pressure to abuse their land. If under the pressure of an adverse economy the soil erodes, soil and water and air are poisoned, the woodlands are wastefully logged, and everything not producing an immediate economic return is neglected, that is apparently understood by most of the society as merely the normal cost of production.

*This means, among other things, that the land and its human communities are not being thought about in places of study and leadership, and this failure to think is causing damage.*But if one lives in a country place, and if one loves it, one must think about it. Under present circumstances, it is not easy to imagine what might be a proper human economy for the country I have just described. And yet, if one loves it, one must make the attempt; if one loves it, the attempt is irresistible.

Two facts are immediately apparent. One is that the present local economy, based like the economies of most rural places exclusively on the export of raw materials, is ruinous. Another is that the influence of a complex, aggressive national economy upon a simple, passive local economy will also be ruinous. In a varied and versatile countryside, fragile in its composition and extremely susceptible to abuse, requiring close human care and elaborate human skills, able to produce and needing to produce a great variety of products from its soils, what is needed, obviously, is a highly diversified local economy.

We should be producing the fullest variety of foods to be consumed locally, in the countryside itself and in nearby towns and cities: meats, grains, table vegetables, fruits and nuts, dairy products, poultry and eggs. We should be harvesting a sustainable yield of fish from our ponds and streams. Our woodlands, managed for continuous yields, selectively and carefully logged, should be yielding a variety of timber for a variety of purposes: firewood, fence posts, lumber for building, fine woods for furniture makers.

And we should be adding value locally to these local products.. What is needed is not the large factory so dear to the hearts of government "developers." To set our whole population to making computers or automobiles would be as gross an error as to use the whole countryside for growing corn or Christmas trees or pulpwood; it would discount everything we have to offer as a community and a place; it would despise our talents and capacities as individuals.

We need, instead, a system of decentralized, small-scale industries to transform the products of our fields and woodlands and streams: small creameries, cheese factories, canneries, grain mills, saw mills, furniture factories, and the like. By "small" I mean simply a size that would not be destructive of the appearance, the health, and the quiet of the countryside. If a factory began to "grow" or to be noisy at night or on Sunday, that would mean that another such factory was needed somewhere else. If waste should occur at any point, that would indicate the need for an enterprise of some other sort. If poison or pollution resulted from any enterprise, that would be understood as an indication that something was absolutely wrong, and a correction would be made. Small scale, of course, makes such changes and corrections more thinkable and more possible than does large scale.

I realize that, by now, my argument has crossed a boundary line of which everyone in our "realistic" society is keenly aware. I will be perceived to have crossed over into "utopianism" or fantasy. Unless I take measures to prevent it, I am going to hear somebody say, "All that would be very nice, if it were possible. Can't you be realistic?"

Well, let me take measures to prevent it. I am not, I admit, optimistic about the success of this kind of thought. Otherwise, my intention, above all, is to be realistic; I wish to be practical. The question here is simply that of convention. Do I want to be realistic according to the conventions of the industrial economy and the military state, or according to what I know of reality? To me, an economy that sees the life of a community or a place as expendable, and reckons its value only in terms of money, is not acceptable because it is *not* realistic. I am thinking as I believe we must think if we wish to discuss the *best* uses of people, places, and things, and if we wish to give affection some standing in our thoughts.

If we wish to make the best use of people, places, and things, then we are going to have to deal with a law that reads about like this: as the quality of use increases, the scale of use (that is, the size of operations) will decline, the tools will become simpler, and the methods and the skills will become more complex. That is a difficult law for us to believe, because we have assumed otherwise for a long time, and yet our experience overwhelmingly suggests that it *is* a law, and that the penalties for disobeying it are severe.

I am making a plea for diversity not only because diversity exists and is pleasant, but also because it is necessary and we need more of it. For an example, let me return to the countryside I described at the beginning of this essay. From birth, I have been familiar with this place and have heard it talked about and thought about. For the last twenty-five years I have been increasingly involved in the use and improvement of a little part of it. As a result of some failures and some successes, I have learned some things about it. I am certain, however, that I do not know the best way to use this land. Nor do I believe that anyone else does. I no longer expect to live to see it come to its best use. But I am beginning to see what is needed, and everywhere the need is for diversity. This is the need of every American rural landscape that I am acquainted with. We need a greater range of species and varieties of plants and animals, of human skills and methods, so that the use may be fitted ever more sensitively and elegantly to the place. Our places, in short, are asking us questions, some of them urgent questions, and we do not have the answers.

The answers, if they are to come and if they are to work, must be developed in the presence of the user and the land; they must be developed to some degree *by* the user *on* the land. The present practice of handing down from on high policies and technologies developed without consideration of the nature and the needs of the land and the people has not worked, and it cannot work. Good agriculture and forestry cannot be "invented" by self-styled smart people in the offices and laboratories of a centralized economy and then sold at the highest possible profit to the supposedly dumb country people. That is not the way good land use comes about. And it does not matter how the methodologies so developed and handed down are labeled; whether "industrial" or "conventional" or "organic" or "sustainable," the professional or professorial condescension that is blind to the primacy of the union between individual people and individual places is ruinous. The challenge to the would-be scientists of an ecologically sane agriculture, as David Ehrenfeld has written, is "to provide unique and particular answers to questions about a farmer's unique and particular land." The proper goal, he adds, is *not* merely to "substitute the cult of the benevolent ecologist for the cult of the benevolent sales representative."

The question of what a beloved country is to be used for quickly becomes inseparable from the questions of who is to use it or who is to prescribe its uses, and what will be the ways of using it. If we speak simply of the use of "a country," then only the first question is asked, and it is asked only by its would-be users. It is not until we speak of "a beloved country"—a particular country, particularly loved—that the question about ways of use will arise. It arises because, loving our country, we see where we are, and we see that present ways of use are not adequate. They are not adequate because such local cultures and economies as we once had have been stunted or destroyed. As a nation, we have attempted to substitute the *concepts* of "land use," "agribusiness," "development," and the like for the *culture* of stewardship and husbandry. And this change is not a result merely of economic pressures and adverse social values; it comes also from the state of affairs in our educational system, especially in our universities.

It is readily evident, once affection is allowed into the discussion of "land use," that the life of the mind, as presently constituted in the universities, is of no help. The sciences are of no help, indeed are destructive, because they work, by principle, outside the demands, checks, and corrections of affection. The problem with this "scientific objectivity" becomes immediately clear when science undertakes to "apply" itself to land use. The problem simply is that land users are using people, places, and things that cannot be well used without affection. To be well used, creatures and places must be used sympathetically, just as they must be known sympathetically to be well known. The economist to whom it is of no concern whether or not a family loves its farm will almost inevitably aid and abet the destruction of family farming. The "animal scientist" to whom it is of no concern whether or not animals suffer will almost inevitably aid and abet the destruction of the decent old ideal of animal husbandry and, as a consequence, increase the suffering of animals. I hope that my country may be delivered from the remote, cold abstractions of university science.

But "the humanities," as presently constituted in the universities, are of no help either, and indeed, with respect to the use of a beloved country, they too have been destructive. (The closer I have come to using the term "humanities," the less satisfactory it has seemed to me; by it I mean everything that is not a "science," another unsatisfactory term.) The humanities have been destructive not because they have been misapplied, but because they have been so frequently understood by their academic stewards as not applicable. The scientific ideals of objectivity and specialization have now crept into the humanities and made themselves at home. This has happened, I think, because the humanities have come to be infected with a suspicion of their uselessness or worthlessness in the face of the provability or workability or profitability of the applied sciences. The conviction is now widespread, for instance, that "a work of art" has no purpose but to be itself. Or if it is allowed that a poem, for instance, has a meaning, then it is a meaning peculiar to its author, its time, or its convention. A poem, in short, is a relic as soon as it is composed; it can be taught, but it cannot teach. The issue of its truth and pertinence is not raised because literary study is conducted with about the same anxiety for "control" as is scientific study. The context of a poem is its text, or the context of its history and criticism as a text. I have not, of course, read all the books or sat in all the classrooms, but my impression is that not much importance is attached to the question of the truth of poems. My impression is that "Comus," for example, is not often taught as an argument with a history and a sequel, with the gravest importance for us in our dilemma now. My impression is that the great works are taught less and less as Ananda Coomaraswamy said they should be: with the recognition "that nothing will have been accomplished unless men's lives are affected and their values changed by what we have to show." My impression is that in the humanities as in the sciences the world is increasingly disallowed as a context. I hope that my country may be delivered from the objectivity of the humanities.

Without a beloved country as context, the arts and the sciences become oriented to the careers of their practitioners, and the intellectual life to intellectual (and bureaucratic) procedures. And so in the universities we see forming an intellectual elite more and more exclusively accomplished in procedures such as promotion, technological innovation, publication, and grant-getting. The context of a beloved country, moreover, implies an academic standard that is not inflatable or deflatable. The standard—the physical, intellectual, political, ecological, economic, and spiritual health of the country—cannot be too high; it will be as high, simply, as we have the love, the vision, and the courage to make it.

I would like my country to be seen and known with an attentiveness that is schooled and skilled. I would like it to be loved with a minutely particular affection and loyalty. I would like the work in it to be practical and loving and respectful and forbearing. In order for these things to happen, the sciences and the humanities are going to have to come together again in the presence of the practical problems of individual places, and of local knowledge and local love in individual people—people able to see, know, think, feel, and act coherently and well without the modern instinct of deference to the "outside expert."

What should the sciences have to say to a citizen in search of the criteria by which to determine the best use of a beloved place or countryside, or of the technical or moral means by which to limit that use to its best use? What should the humanities have to say to a scientist—or, for that matter, a citizen—in search of the cultural instructions that might effectively govern the use of a beloved place? These questions or such questions could reunite the sciences and the humanities. That a scientist and an artist can speak and work together in response to such questions I know from my own experience. All that is necessary is a mutuality of concern and a mutual willingness to speak common English. When friends speak across these divisions or out of their "departments," in mutual concern for a beloved country, then it is clear that these diverse disciplines are not "competing interests," as the university structure and academic folklore suggest, but interests with legitimate claims on all minds. It is only when the country becomes an abstraction, a prize of conquest, that these interests compete—though, of course, when that has happened *all* interests compete.

But in order to assure that a beloved country might be lovingly used, the sciences and the humanities will have to do more than mend their divorce at "the university level"; they will also have to mend their divorce from the common culture, by which I do not mean the "popular culture," but rather the low and local wisdom that is now either relegated to the compartments of anthropology or folklore or "oral history," or not attended to at all.

Some time ago, after I had given a lecture at a college in Ohio, a gentleman came up and introduced himself to me as a fellow Kentuckian.

"Where in Kentucky are you from?" I asked

"Oh, a little place you probably never heard of—North Middletown."

"I *have* heard of North Middletown," I said. "It was the home of my father's great friend John W. Jones."

"Well, John W. Jones was my uncle."

I told him then of my father's and my own respect for Mr. Jones.

"I want to tell you a story about Uncle John," he said. And he told me this:

When his Uncle John was president of the bank in North Middletown, his policy was to give a loan to any graduate of the North Middletown high school who wanted to go to college and needed the money. This practice caused great consternation to the bank examiners who came and found those unsecured loans on the books and no justification for them except Mr. Jones's conviction that it was right to make them.

As it turned out, it was right in more than principle, for in the many years that Mr. Jones was president of the bank, making those "unsound loans," *all* of the loans were repaid; he never lost a dime on a one of them.

I do not mean to raise here the question of the invariable goodness of a college education, which I doubt. My point in telling this story is that Mr. Jones was acting from a kind of knowledge, inestimably valuable and probably indispensable, that comes out of common culture and that cannot be taught as a part of the formal curriculum of a school. The students whose education he enabled were not taught this knowledge at the colleges they attended. What he knew—and this involved his knowledge of himself, his tradition, his community, and everybody in it—was that trust, in the circumstances then present, could beget trustworthiness. This is the kind of knowledge, obviously, that is fundamental to the possibility of community life and to certain good possibilities in the characters of people. Though I don't believe that it can be taught and learned in a university, I think that it should be known about and respected in a university, and I don't know where, in the sciences and the humanities as presently constituted, students would be led to suspect, much less to honor, its existence. It is certainly no part of banking or of economics as now taught and practiced. It is a part of community life, which most scientists ignore in their professional pursuits, and which most people in the humanities seem to regard as belonging to a past now useless or lost or dispensed with.

Let me give another, more fundamental example. My brother, who is a lawyer, recently had as a client an elderly man named Bennie Yeary who had farmed for many years a farm of about three hundred acres of hilly and partly forested land. His farm and the road to his house had been damaged by a power company.

Seeking to determine the value of the land, my brother asked him if he had ever logged his woodlands. Mr. Yeary answered, "Yes, sir, since 1944. . . . I have never robbed [the land]. I have always just cut a little out where I thought it needed it. I have got as much timber right now, I am satisfied, . . . as I had when I started mill runs here in '44."

That we should not rob the land is a principle to be found readily enough in the literary culture. That it came into literature out of the common culture is suggested by the fact that it is commonly phrased in this way by people who have not inherited the literary culture. That we should not rob the land, anyhow, is a principle that can be learned from books. But the ways of living on the land so as not to rob it probably cannot be learned from books, and this is made clear by a further exchange between my brother and Mr. Yeary.

They came to the question of what was involved in the damage to the road, and the old farmer said that the power company had destroyed thirteen or fourteen water breaks. A water break is a low mound of rock and earth built to divert the water out of a hilly road. It is a means of preventing erosion both of the roadbed and of the land alongside it, one of the ways of living on the land without robbing it.

"How long . . . had it been since you had those water breaks constructed in there?"

"I had been working on them . . . off and on, for about twelve years, putting them water breaks in. I hauled rocks out of my fields . . . and I would dig out, bury these rocks down, and take the sledgehammer and beat rock in here and make this water break."

The way to make a farm road that will not rob the land cannot be learned from books, then, because the long use of such a road is a part of the proper way of making it, and because the use and improvement of the road are intimately involved with the use and improvement of the place. It is of the utmost importance that the rocks to make the water breaks were hauled from the fields. Mr. Yeary's solution did not, like the typical industrial solution, involve the making of a problem, or a series of problems, elsewhere. It involved the making of a solution elsewhere: the same work that improved the road improved the fields. Such work requires not only correct principles, skill, and industry, but a knowledge of local particulars and many years; it involves slow, small adjustments in response to questions asked by a particular place. And this is true in general of the patterns and structures of a proper human use of a beloved country, as examination of the traditional landscapes of the Old World will readily show: they were made by use as much as by skill.

This implication of use in the making of essential artifacts and the maintenance of the landscape—which are to so large an extent the making and the maintenance of culture—brings us to the inescapable final step in an argument for diversity: the realization that without a diversity of people we cannot maintain a diversity of anything else. By a diversity of people I do not mean a diversity of specialists, but a diversity of people elegantly suited to live in their places and to bring them to their best use, whether the use is that of uselessness, as in a place left wild, or that of the highest sustainable productivity. The most abundant diversity of creatures and ways cannot be maintained in preserves, zoos, museums, and the like, but only in the occupations and the pleasures of an appropriately diversified human economy.

The proper ways of using a beloved country are "humanities," I think, and are as complex, difficult, interesting, and worthy as any of the rest. But they defy the present intellectual and academic categories. They are *both* science and art, knowing and doing. Indispensable as these ways are to the success of human life, they have no place and no standing in the present structures of our intellectual life. The purpose, indeed, of the present structures of our intellectual life has been to educate them out of existence. I think I know where in any university my brother's client, Mr. Yeary, would be laughed at or ignored or tape-recorded or classified. I don't know where he would be appropriately honored. The scientific disciplines certainly do not honor him, and the "humane" ones almost as certainly do not. We would have to go some distance back in the literary tradition—back to Thomas Hardy at least, and before Hardy to Wordsworth—to find the due respect paid to such a person. He *has* been educated almost out of existence, and yet an understanding of his importance and worth would renew the life of the mind in this country, in the university and out.

1988

WHAT ARE
PEOPLE FOR?

Since World War II, the governing agricultural doctrine in government offices, universities, and corporations has been that "there are too many people on the farm." This idea has supported, if indeed it has not caused, one of the most consequential migrations of history: millions of rural people moving from country to city in a stream that has not slackened from the war's end until now. And the strongest force behind this migration, then as now, has been economic ruin on the farm. Today, with hundreds of farm families losing their farms every week, the economists are still saying, as they have said all along, that these people deserve to fail, that they have failed because they are the "least efficient producers," and that the rest of us are better off for their failure.

It is apparently easy to say that there are too many farmers, if one is not a farmer. This is not a pronouncement often heard in farm communities. Nor have farmers yet been informed of a dangerous surplus of population in the "agribusiness" professions or among the middlemen of the food system. No agricultural economist has yet perceived that there are too many agricultural economists.

The farm-to-city migration has obviously produced advantages to the corporate economy. The absent farmers have had to be replaced by machinery, petroleum, chemicals, credit, and other expensive goods and services from the agribusiness economy, which ought not to be confused with the economy of what used to be called farming.

But these short-term advantages all imply long-term disadvantages, to both country and city. The departure of so many people has seriously weakened rural communities and economies all over the country. And that our farmland no longer has enough caretakers is implied by the fact that, as the farming people have departed from the land, the land itself has departed. Our soil erosion rates are now higher than they were in the time of the Dust Bowl.

At the same time, the cities have had to receive a great influx of people unprepared for urban life and unable to cope with it. A friend of mine, a psychologist who has frequently worked with the juvenile courts in a large midwestern city, has told me that a major occupation of the police force there is to keep the "permanently unemployable" confined in their own part of town. Such a circumstance cannot be good for the future of democracy and freedom. One wonders what the authors of our Constitution would have thought of that category, "permanently unemployable."

Equally important is the question of the sustainability of the urban food supply. The supermarkets are, at present, crammed with food, and the productivity of American agriculture is, at present, enormous. But this is a productivity based on the ruin both of the producers and of the source of production. City people are unworried about this, apparently, only because they do not know anything about farming. People who know about farming, who know what the farmland requires to remain productive, *are* worried. When topsoil losses exceed the weight of grain harvested fivefold (in Iowa) or twentyfold (in the wheatlands of eastern Washington), there is something to worry about.

When the "too many" of the country arrive in the city, they are not called "too many." In the city they are called "unemployed" or "permanently unemployable." But what will happen if the economists ever perceive that there are too many people in the cities? There appear to be only two possibilities: either they will have to recognize that their earlier diagnosis was a tragic error, or they will conclude that there are too many people in country and city both—and what further inhumanities will be justified by *that* diagnosis?

The great question that hovers over this issue, one that we have dealt with mainly by indifference, is the question of what people are *for*. Is their greatest dignity in unemployment? Is the obsolescence of human beings now our social goal? One would conclude so from our attitude toward work, especially the manual work necessary to the long-term preservation of the land, and from our rush toward mechanization, automation, and computerization. In a country that puts an absolute premium on labor-saving measures, short workdays, and retirement, why should there be any surprise at permanence of unemployment and welfare dependency? Those are only different names for our national ambitions.

In the country, meanwhile, there is work to be done. This is the inescapably necessary work of restoring and caring for our farms, forests, and rural towns and communities—work that we have not been able to pay people to do for forty years and that, thanks to our forty-year "solution to the farm problem," few people any longer know how to do.

1985

WASTE

As a country person, I often feel that I am on the bottom end of the waste problem. I live on the Kentucky River about ten miles from its entrance into the Ohio. The Kentucky, in many ways a lovely river, receives an abundance of pollution from the Eastern Kentucky coal mines and the central Kentucky cities. When the river rises, it carries a continuous raft of cans, bottles, plastic jugs, chunks of styrofoam, and other imperishable trash. After the floods subside, I, like many other farmers, must pick up the trash before I can use my bottomland fields. I have seen the Ohio, whose name (*Oyo* in Iroquois) means "beautiful river," so choked with this manufactured filth that an ant could crawl dry-footed from Kentucky to Indiana. The air of both river valleys is seriously polluted. Our roadsides and roadside fields lie under a constant precipitation of cans, bottles, the plastic-ware of fast food joints, soiled plastic diapers, and sometimes whole bags of garbage. In our county we now have a "sanitary landfill" which daily receives, in addition to our local production, fifty to sixty large truckloads of garbage from Pennsylvania, New Jersey, and New York.

Moreover, a close inspection of our countryside would reveal, strewn over it from one end to the other, thousands of derelict and worthless automobiles, house trailers, refrigerators, stoves, freezers, washing machines, and dryers; as well as thousands of unregulated dumps in hollows and sink holes, on streambanks and roadsides, filled not only with "disposable" containers but also with broken toasters, television sets, toys of all kinds, furniture, lamps, stereos, radios, scales, coffee makers, mixers, blenders, corn poppers, hair dryers, and microwave ovens. Much of our waste problem is to be accounted for by the intentional flimsiness and unrepairability of the labor-savers and gadgets that we have become addicted to.

Of course, my sometime impression that I live on the receiving end of this problem is false, for country people contribute their full share. The truth is that we Americans, all of us, have become a kind of human trash, living our lives in the midst of a ubiquitous damned mess of which we are at once the victims and the perpetrators. We are all unwilling victims, perhaps; and some of us even are unwilling perpetrators, but we must count ourselves among the guilty nonetheless. In my household we produce much of our own food and try to do without as many frivolous "necessities" as possible—and yet, like everyone else, we must shop, and when we shop we must bring home a load of plastic, aluminum, and glass containers designed to be thrown away, and "appliances" designed to wear out quickly and be thrown away.

I confess that I am angry at the manufacturers who make these things. There are days when I would be delighted if certain corporation executives could somehow be obliged to eat their products. I know of no good reason why these containers and all other forms of manufactured "waste"—solid, liquid, toxic, or whatever—should not be outlawed. There is no sense and no sanity in objecting to the desecration of the flag while tolerating and justifying and encouraging as a daily business the desecration of the country for which it stands.

But our waste problem is not the fault only of producers. It is the fault of an economy that is wasteful from top to bottom—a symbiosis of an unlimited greed at the top and a lazy, passive, and self-indulgent consumptiveness at the bottom—and all of us are involved in it. If we wish to correct this economy, we must be careful to understand and to demonstrate how much waste of human life is involved in our waste of the material goods of Creation. For example, much of the litter that now defaces our country is fairly directly caused by the massive secession or exclusion of most of our people from active participation in the food economy. We have made a social ideal of minimal involvement in the growing and cooking of food. This is one of the dearest "liberations" of our affluence. Nevertheless, the more dependent we become on the *industries* of eating and drinking, the more waste we are going to produce. The mess that surrounds us, then, must be understood not just as a problem in itself but as a symptom of a greater and graver problem: the centralization of our economy, the gathering of the productive property and power into fewer and fewer hands, and the consequent destruction, everywhere, of the local economies of household, neighborhood, and community.

This is the source of our unemployment problem, and I am not talking just about the unemployment of eligible members of the "labor force." I mean also the unemployment of children and old people, who, in viable household and local economies, would have work to do by which they would be useful to themselves and to others. The ecological damage of centralization and waste is thus inextricably involved with human damage. For we have, as a result, not only a desecrated, ugly, and dangerous country in which to live until we are in some manner poisoned by it, and a constant and now generally accepted problem of unemployed or unemployable workers, but also classrooms full of children who lack the experience and discipline of fundamental human tasks, and various institutions full of still capable old people who are useless and lonely.

I think that we must learn to see the trash on our streets and roadsides, in our rivers, and in our woods and fields, not as the side effects of "more jobs" as its manufacturers invariably insist that it is, but as evidence of good work *not* done by people able to do it.

1989

ECONOMY

AND PLEASURE

To those who still uphold the traditions of religious and political thought that influenced the shaping of our society and the founding of our government, it is astonishing, and of course discouraging, to see economics now elevated to the position of ultimate justifier and explainer of all the affairs of our daily life, and competition enshrined as the sovereign principle and ideal of economics.

As thousands of small farms and small local businesses of all kinds falter and fail under the effects of adverse economic policies or live under the threat of what we complacently call "scientific progress," the economist sits in the calm of professorial tenure and government subsidy, commenting and explaining for the illumination of the press and the general public. If those who fail happen to be fellow humans, neighbors, children of God, and citizens of the republic, all that is outside the purview of the economist. As the farmers go under, as communities lose their economic supports, as all of rural America sits as if condemned in the shadow of the "free market" and "revolutionary science," the economist announces pontifically to the press that "there will be some winners and some losers"—as if that might justify and clarify everything, or anything. The sciences, one gathers, mindlessly serve economics, and the humanities defer abjectly to the sciences. All assume, apparently, that we are in the grip of the determination of economic laws that are the laws of the universe. The newspapers quote the economists as the ultimate authorities. We read their pronouncements, knowing that the last word has been said.

"Science," President Reagan says, "tells us that the break-throughs in superconductivity bring us to the threshold of a new age." He is speaking to "a federal conference on the commercial applications of the new technology," and we know that by "science" he means scientists in the pay of corporations. "It is our task at this conference," he says, "to herald in that new age with a rush." A part of his program to accomplish this task is a proposal to "relax" the antitrust laws.* Thus even the national executive and our legal system itself must now defer to the demands of "the economy." Whatever "new age" is at hand at the moment must be heralded in "with a rush" because of the profits available to those who will rush it in.

It seems that we have been reduced almost to a state of absolute economics, in which people and all other creatures and things may be considered purely as economic "units," or integers of production, and in which a human being may be dealt with, as John Ruskin put it, "merely as a covetous machine."† And the voices bitterest to hear are those saying that all this destructive work of mindless genius, money, and power is regrettable but cannot be helped.

Perhaps it cannot. Surely we would be fools if, having understood the logic of this terrible process, we assumed that it might not go on in its glutton's optimism until it achieves the catastrophe that is its logical end. But let us suppose that a remedy is possible. If so, perhaps the best beginning would be in understanding the falseness and silliness of the economic ideal of competition, which is destructive both of nature and of human nature because it is untrue to both.

The ideal of competition always implies, and in fact requires, that any community must be divided into a class of winners and a class of losers. This division is radically different from other so-

---

*"Reagan calls for effort to find commercial uses for superconductors," *Louisville Courier-Journal*, July 29, 1987, p. A3.
†John Ruskin, *Unto This Last* (Lincoln: University of Nebraska Press, 1967), p. 11.

cial divisions: that of the more able and the less able, or that of the richer and the poorer, or even that of the rulers and the ruled. These latter divisions have existed throughout history and at times, at least, have been ameliorated by social and religious ideals that instructed the strong to help the weak. As a purely economic ideal, competition does not contain or imply any such instructions. In fact, the defenders of the ideal of competition have never known what to do with or for the losers. The losers simply accumulate in human dumps, like stores of industrial waste, until they gain enough misery and strength to overpower the winners. The idea that the displaced and dispossessed "should seek retraining and get into another line of work" is, of course, utterly cynical; it is only the hand-washing practiced by officials and experts.* A loser, by definition, is somebody whom nobody knows what to do with. There is no limit to the damage and the suffering implicit in this willingness that losers should exist as a normal economic cost.

The danger of the ideal of competition is that it neither proposes nor implies any limits. It proposes simply to lower costs at any cost, and to raise profits at any cost. It does not hesitate at the destruction of the life of a family or the life of a community. It pits neighbor against neighbor as readily as it pits buyer against seller. Every transaction is *meant* to involve a winner and a loser. And for this reason the human economy is pitted without limit against nature. For in the unlimited competition of neighbor and neighbor, buyer and seller, all available means must be used; none may be spared.

I will be told that indeed there are limits to economic competitiveness as now practiced—that, for instance, one is not allowed to kill one's competitor. But, leaving aside the issue of whether or not murder would be acceptable as an economic means if the stakes were high enough, it is a fact that the destruction of life is a part of the daily business of economic competition as now prac-

*Reed Karaim, "Loss of million farms in 14 years projected," *Des Moines Register*, March 18, 1986, p. 1A.

ticed. If one person is willing to take another's property or to accept another's ruin as a normal result of economic enterprise, then he is willing to destroy that other person's life as it is and as it desires to be. That this person's biological existence has been spared seems merely incidental; it was spared because it was not worth anything. That this person is now "free" to "seek retraining and get into another line of work" signifies only that his life as it was has been destroyed.

But there is another implication in the limitlessness of the ideal of competition that is politically even more ominous: namely, that unlimited economic competitiveness proposes an unlimited concentration of economic power. Economic anarchy, like any other free-for-all, tends inevitably toward dominance by the strongest. If it is normal for economic activity to divide the community into a class of winners and a class of losers, then the inescapable implication is that the class of winners will become ever smaller, the class of losers ever larger. And that, obviously, is now happening: the usable property of our country, once divided somewhat democratically, is owned by fewer and fewer people every year. That the president of the republic can, without fear, propose the "relaxation" of antitrust laws in order to "rush" the advent of a commercial "new age" suggests not merely that we are "rushing" toward plutocracy, but that this is now a permissible goal for the would-be winning class for which Mr. Reagan speaks and acts, and a burden acceptable to nearly everybody else.

Nowhere, I believe, has this grossly oversimplified version of economics made itself more at home than in the land-grant universities. The colleges of agriculture, for example, having presided over the now nearly completed destruction of their constituency—the farm people and the farm communities—are now scrambling to ally themselves more firmly than ever, not with "the rural home and rural life"* that were, and are, their trust, but with the technocratic aims and corporate interests that

*This is the language of the Hatch Act, *United States Code*, Section 361b.

are destroying the rural home and rural life. This, of course, is only a new intensification of an old alliance. The revolution that began with machines and chemicals proposes now to continue with automation, computers, and biotechnology. That this has been and is a revolution is undeniable. It has not been merely a "scientific revolution," as its proponents sometimes like to call it, but also an economic one, involving great and profound changes in property ownership and the distribution of real wealth. It has done by insidious tendency what the communist revolutions have done by fiat: it has dispossessed the people and usurped the power and integrity of community life.

This work has been done, and is still being done, under the heading of altruism: its aims, as its proponents never tire of repeating, are to "serve agriculture" and to "feed the world." These aims, as stated, are irreproachable; as pursued, they raise a number of doubts. Agriculture, it turns out, is to be served strictly according to the rules of competitive economics. The aim is "to make farmers more competitive" and "to make American agriculture more competitive." Against whom, we must ask, are our farmers and our agriculture to be made more competitive? And we must answer, because we know: Against other farmers, at home and abroad. Now, if the colleges of agriculture "serve agriculture" by helping farmers to compete against one another, what do they propose to do to help the farmers who have been out-competed? Well, those people are not farmers anymore, and therefore are of no concern to the academic servants of agriculture. Besides, they are the beneficiaries of the inestimable liberty to "seek retraining and get into another line of work."

And so the colleges of agriculture, entrusted though they are to serve the rural home and rural life, give themselves over to a hysterical rhetoric of "change," "the future," "the frontiers of modern science," "competition," "the competitive edge," "the cutting edge," "early adoption," and the like, as if there is nothing worth learning from the past and nothing worth preserving in the present. The idea of the teacher and scholar as one called upon to preserve and pass on a common cultural and natural birthright has been almost entirely replaced by the idea of the teacher and scholar as a developer of "human capital" and a bestower of economic advantage. The ambition is to make the university an "economic resource" in a competition for wealth and power that is local, national, and global. Of course, all this works directly against the rural home and rural life, because it works directly against community.

There is no denying that competitiveness is a part of the life both of an individual and of a community, or that, within limits, it is a useful and necessary part. But it is equally obvious that no individual can lead a good or a satisfying life under the rule of competition, and that no community can succeed except by limiting somehow the competitiveness of its members. One cannot maintain one's "competitive edge" if one helps other people. The advantage of "early adoption" would disappear—it would not be thought of—in a community that put a proper value on mutual help. Such advantages would not be thought of by people intent on loving their neighbors as themselves. And it is impossible to imagine that there can be any reconciliation between local and national competitiveness and global altruism. The ambition to "feed the world" or "feed the hungry," rising as it does out of the death struggle of farmer with farmer, proposes not the filling of stomachs, but the engorgement of "the bottom line." The strangest of all the doctrines of the cult of competition, in which admittedly there must be losers as well as winners, is that the result of competition is inevitably good for everybody, that altruistic ends may be met by a system without altruistic motives or altruistic means.

In agriculture, competitiveness has been based throughout the industrial era on constantly accelerating technological change—the very *principle* of agricultural competitiveness is ever-accelerating change—and this has encouraged an ever-accelerating dependency on purchased products, products purchased ever farther from home. Community, however, aspires toward stability. It strives to balance change with constancy. That is why community life places such high value on neighborly love, marital fidelity, local loyalty, the integrity and continuity of family life, respect for the old, and instruction of the young. And a vital community draws its life, so far as possible, from local sources. It prefers to solve its problems, for example, by non-monetary exchanges of help, not by buying things. A community cannot survive under the rule of competition.

But the land-grant universities, in espousing the economic determinism of the industrialists, have caught themselves in a logical absurdity that they may finally discover to be dangerous to themselves. If competitiveness is the economic norm, and the "competitive edge" the only recognized social goal, then how can these institutions justify public support? Why, in other words, should the public be willing to permit a corporation to profit privately from research that has been subsidized publicly? Why should not the industries be required to afford their own research, and why should not the laws of competition and the free market—if indeed they perform as advertised—enable industries to do their own research a great deal more cheaply than the universities can do it?

The question that we finally come to is a practical one, though it is not one that is entirely answerable by empirical methods: Can a university, or a nation, *afford* this exclusive rule of competition, this purely economic economy? The great fault of this approach to things is that it is so drastically reductive; it does not permit us to live and work as human beings, as the best of our inheritance defines us. Rats and roaches live by competition under the law of supply and demand; it is the privilege of human beings to live under the laws of justice and mercy. It is impossible not to notice how little the proponents of the ideal of competition have to say about honesty, which is the fundamental economic virtue, and how *very* little they have to say about community, compassion, and mutual help.

But what the ideal of competition most flagrantly and disastrously excludes is affection. The affections, John Ruskin said, are "an anomalous force, rendering every one of the ordinary political economist's calculations nugatory; while, even if he desired to introduce this new element into his estimates, he has no power of dealing with it; for the affections only become a true motive power when they ignore every other motive power and condition of political economy."* Thus, if we are sane, we do not dismiss or abandon our infant children or our aged parents because they are too young or too old to work. For human beings, affection is the ultimate motive, because the force that powers us, as Ruskin also said, is not "steam, magnetism, or gravitation," but "a Soul."

I would like now to attempt to talk about economy from the standpoint of affection—or, as I am going to call it, pleasure, advancing just a little beyond Ruskin's term, for pleasure is, so to speak, affection in action. There are obvious risks in approaching an economic problem by a way that is frankly emotional—to talk, for example, about the pleasures of nature and the pleasures of work. But these risks seem to me worth taking, for what I am trying to deal with here is the grief that we increasingly suffer as a result of the loss of those pleasures.

It is necessary, at the outset, to make a distinction between pleasure that is true or legitimate and pleasure that is not. We know that a pleasure can be as heavily debited as an economy. Some people undoubtedly thought it pleasant, for example, to have the most onerous tasks of their economy performed by black slaves. But this proved to be a pleasure that was temporary and dangerous. It lived by an enormous indebtedness that was inescapably to be paid not in money, but in misery, waste, and death. The pleasures of fossil fuel combustion and nuclear "security" are, as we are beginning to see, similarly debited to the future. These pleasures are in every way analogous to the self-indulgent pleasures of individuals. They are pleasures that we are

*Ruskin, *Unto This Last*, p. 16.

allowed to have merely to the extent that we can ignore or defer the logical consequences.

That there is pleasure in competition is not to be doubted. We know from childhood that winning is fun. But we probably begin to grow up when we begin to sympathize with the loser—that is, when we begin to understand that competition involves costs as well as benefits. Sometimes perhaps, as in the most innocent games, the benefits are all to the winner and the costs all to the loser. But when the competition is more serious, when the stakes are higher and greater power is used, then we know that the winner shares in the cost, sometimes disastrously. In war, for example, even the winner is a loser. And this is equally true of our present economy: in unlimited economic competition, the winners are losers; that they may appear to be winners is owing only to their temporary ability to charge their costs to other people or to nature.

But a victory over community or nature can be won only at everybody's cost. For example, we now have in the United States many landscapes that have been defeated—temporarily or permanently—by strip mining, by clear-cutting, by poisoning, by bad farming, or by various styles of "development" that have subjugated their sites entirely to human purposes. These landscapes have been defeated for the benefit of what are assumed to be victorious landscapes: the suburban housing developments and the places of amusement (the park systems, the recreational wildernesses) of the winners—so far—in the economy. But these victorious landscapes and their human inhabitants are already paying the costs of their defeat of other landscapes: in air and water pollution, overcrowding, inflated prices, and various diseases of body and mind. Eventually, the cost will be paid in scarcity or want of necessary goods.

Is it possible to look beyond this all-consuming "rush" of winning and losing to the possibility of countrysides, a nation of countrysides, in which use is not synonymous with defeat? It is. But in order to do so we must consider our pleasures. Since we all know, from our own and our nation's experience, of some pleasures that are canceled by their costs, and of some that result in unredeemable losses and miseries, it is natural to wonder if there may not be such phenomena as *net* pleasures, pleasures that are free or without a permanent cost. And we know that there are. These are the pleasures that we take in our own lives, our own wakefulness in this world, and in the company of other people and other creatures—pleasures innate in the Creation and in our own good work. It is in these pleasures that we possess the likeness to God that is spoken of in Genesis.

"This curious world we inhabit is more wonderful than convenient; more beautiful than it is useful; it is more to be admired and enjoyed than used."* Henry David Thoreau said that to his graduating class at Harvard in 1837. We may assume that to most of them it sounded odd, as to most of the Harvard graduating class of 1987 it undoubtedly still would. But perhaps we will be encouraged to take him seriously, if we recognize that this idea is not something that Thoreau made up out of thin air. When he uttered it, he may very well have been remembering Revelation 4:11: "Thou art worthy, O Lord, to receive glory and honour and power: for thou hast created all things, and for thy pleasure they are and were created." That God created "all things" is in itself an uncomfortable thought, for in our workaday world we can hardly avoid preferring some things above others, and this makes it hard to imagine *not* doing so. That God created all things for His pleasure, and that they continue to exist because they please Him, is formidable doctrine indeed, as far as possible both from the "anthropocentric" utilitarianism that some environmentalist critics claim to find in the Bible and from the grouchy spirituality of many Christians.

It would be foolish, probably, to suggest that God's pleasure in all things can be fully understood or appreciated by mere

* *Familiar Letters of Henry David Thoreau*, ed. F. B. Sanborn (Boston and New York: Houghton Mifflin, 1894), p. 9.

humans. The passage suggests, however, that our truest and profoundest religious experience may be the simple, unasking pleasure in the existence of other creatures that *is* possible to humans. It suggests that God's pleasure in all things must be respected by us in our use of things, and even in our displeasure in some things. It suggests too that we have an obligation to preserve God's pleasure in all things, and surely this means not only that we must not misuse or abuse anything, but also that there must be some things and some places that by common agreement we do not use at all, but leave wild. This bountiful and lovely thought that all creatures are pleasing to God—and potentially pleasing, therefore, to us—is unthinkable from the point of view of an economy divorced from pleasure, such as the one we have now, which completely discounts the capacity of people to be affectionate toward what they do and what they use and where they live and the other people and creatures with whom they live.

It may be argued that our whole society is more devoted to pleasure than any whole society ever was in the past, that we support in fact a great variety of pleasure industries and that these are thriving as never before. But that would seem only to prove my point. That there can be pleasure industries at all, exploiting our apparently limitless inability to be pleased, can only mean that our economy is divorced from pleasure and that pleasure is gone from our workplaces and our dwelling places. Our workplaces are more and more exclusively given over to production, and our dwelling places to consumption. And this accounts for the accelerating division of our country into defeated landscapes and victorious (but threatened) landscapes.

More and more, we take for granted that work must be destitute of pleasure. More and more, we assume that if we want to be pleased we must wait until evening, or the weekend, or vacation, or retirement. More and more, our farms and forests resemble our factories and offices, which in turn more and more resemble prisons—why else should we be so eager to escape them? We recognize defeated landscapes by the absence of pleasure from them. We are defeated at work because our work gives us no pleasure. We are defeated at home because we have no pleasant work there. We turn to the pleasure industries for relief from our defeat, and are again defeated, for the pleasure industries can thrive and grow only upon our dissatisfaction with them.

Where is our comfort but in the free, uninvolved, finally mysterious beauty and grace of this world that we did not make, that has no price? Where is our sanity but there? Where is our pleasure but in working and resting kindly in the presence of this world?

And in the right sort of economy, our pleasure would not be merely an addition or by-product or reward; it would be both an empowerment of our work and its indispensable measure. Pleasure, Ananda Coomaraswamy said, *perfects* work. In order to have leisure and pleasure, we have mechanized and automated and computerized our work. But what does this do but divide us ever more from our work and our products—and, in the process, from one another and the world? What have farmers done when they have mechanized and computerized their farms? They have removed themselves and their pleasure from their work.

I was fortunate, late in his life, to know Henry Besuden of Clark County, Kentucky, the premier Southdown sheep breeder and one of the great farmers of his time. He told me once that his first morning duty in the spring and early summer was to saddle his horse and ride across his pastures to see the condition of the grass when it was freshest from the moisture and coolness of the night. What he wanted to see in his pastures at that time of year, when his spring lambs would be fattening, was what he called "bloom"—by which he meant not flowers, but a certain visible delectability. He recognized it, of course, by his delight in it. He was one of the best of the traditional livestockmen—the husbander or husband of his animals. As such, he was not interested in "statistical indicators" of his flock's "productivity." He wanted his sheep to be pleased. If they were pleased with their pasture, they would eat eagerly, drink well, rest, and grow. He knew their pleasure by his own.

The nearly intolerable irony in our dissatisfaction is that we have removed pleasure from our work in order to remove "drudgery" from our lives. If I could pick any rule of industrial economics to receive a thorough re-examination by our people, it would be the one that says that all hard physical work is "drudgery" and not worth doing. There are of course many questions surrounding this issue: What is the work? In whose interest is it done? Where and in what circumstances is it done? How well and to what result is it done? In whose company is it done? How long does it last? And so forth. But this issue is personal and so needs to be re-examined by everybody. The argument, if it is that, can proceed only by personal testimony.

I can say, for example, that the tobacco harvest in my own home country involves the hardest work that I have done in any quantity. In most of the years of my life, from early boyhood until now, I have taken part in the tobacco cutting. This work usually occurs at some time between the last part of August and the first part of October. Usually the weather is hot; usually we are in a hurry. The work is extremely demanding, and often, because of the weather, it has the character of an emergency. Because all of the work still must be done by hand, this event has maintained much of its old character; it is very much the sort of thing the agriculture experts have had in mind when they have talked about freeing people from drudgery.

That the tobacco cutting *can* be drudgery is obvious. If there is too much of it, if it goes on too long, if one has no interest in it, if one cannot reconcile oneself to the misery involved in it, if one does not like or enjoy the company of one's fellow workers, then drudgery would be the proper name for it.

But for me, and I think for most of the men and women who have been my companions in this work, it has not been drudgery.

None of us would say that we take pleasure in all of it all of the time, but we do take pleasure in it, and sometimes the pleasure can be intense and clear. Many of my dearest memories come from these times of hardest work.

The tobacco cutting is the most protracted social occasion of our year. Neighbors work together; they are together all day every day for weeks. The quiet of the work is not much interrupted by machine noises, and so there is much talk. There is the talk involved in the management of the work. There is incessant speculation about the weather. There is much laughter; because of the unrelenting difficulty of the work, everything funny or amusing is relished. And there are memories.

The crew to which I belong is the product of kinships and friendships going far back; my own earliest associations with it occurred nearly forty years ago. And so as we work we have before us not only the present crop and the present fields, but other crops and other fields that are remembered. The tobacco cutting is a sort of ritual of remembrance. Old stories are re-told; the dead and the absent are remembered. Some of the best talk I have ever listened to I have heard during these times, and I am especially moved to think of the care that is sometimes taken to speak well—that is, to speak fittingly—of the dead and the absent. The conversation, one feels, is ancient. Such talk in barns and at row ends must go back without interruption to the first farmers. How long it may continue is now an uneasy question; not much longer perhaps, but we do not know. We only know that while it lasts it can carry us deeply into our shared life and the happiness of farming.

On many days we have had somebody's child or somebody's children with us, playing in the barn or around the patch while we worked, and these have been our best days. One of the most regrettable things about the industrialization of work is the segregation of children. As industrial work excludes the dead by social mobility and technological change, it excludes children by haste and danger. The small scale and the handwork of our tobacco cutting permit margins both temporal and spatial that accommodate the play of children. The children play at the grownups' work, as well as at their own play. In their play the children learn to work; they learn to know their elders and their country. And the presence of playing children means invariably that the grown-ups play too from time to time.

(I am perforce aware of the problems and the controversies about tobacco. I have spoken of the tobacco harvest here simply because it is the only remaining farm job in my part of the country that still involves a traditional neighborliness.)

Ultimately, in the argument about work and how it should be done, one has only one's pleasure to offer. It is possible, as I have learned again and again, to be in one's place, in such company, wild or domestic, and with such pleasure, that one cannot think of another place that one would prefer to be—or of another place at all. One does not miss or regret the past, or fear or long for the future. Being there is simply all, and is enough. Such times give one the chief standard and the chief reason for one's work.

Last December, when my granddaughter, Katie, had just turned five, she stayed with me one day while the rest of the family was away from home. In the afternoon we hitched a team of horses to the wagon and hauled a load of dirt for the barn floor. It was a cold day, but the sun was shining; we hauled our load of dirt over the tree-lined gravel lane beside the creek—a way well known to her mother and to my mother when they were children. As we went along, Katie drove the team for the first time in her life. She did very well, and she was proud of herself. She said that her mother would be proud of her, and I said that I was proud of her.

We completed our trip to the barn, unloaded our load of dirt, smoothed it over the barn floor, and wetted it down. By the time we started back up the creek road the sun had gone over the hill and the air had turned bitter. Katie sat close to me in the wagon, and we did not say anything for a long time. I did not say anything because I was afraid that Katie was not saying anything because she was cold and tired and miserable and perhaps homesick; it was impossible to hurry much, and I was unsure how I would comfort her.

But then, after a while, she said, "Wendell, isn't it fun?"

1988

THE PLEASURES

OF EATING

Many times, after I have finished a lecture on the decline of American farming and rural life, someone in the audience has asked, "What can city people do?"

"Eat responsibly," I have usually answered. Of course, I have tried to explain what I meant by that, but afterwards I have invariably felt that there was more to be said than I had been able to say. Now I would like to attempt a better explanation.

I begin with the proposition that eating is an agricultural act. Eating ends the annual drama of the food economy that begins with planting and birth. Most eaters, however, are no longer aware that this is true. They think of food as an agricultural product, perhaps, but they do not think of themselves as participants in agriculture. They think of themselves as "consumers." If they think beyond that, they recognize that they are passive consumers. They buy what they want—or what they have been persuaded to want—within the limits of what they can get. They pay, mostly without protest, what they are charged. And they mostly ignore certain critical questions about the quality and the cost of what they are sold: How fresh is it? How pure or clean is it, how free of dangerous chemicals? How far was it transported, and what did transportation add to the cost? How much did manufacturing or packaging or advertising add to the cost? When the food product has been manufactured or "processed" or "precooked," how has that affected its quality or price or nutritional value?

Most urban shoppers would tell you that food is produced on farms. But most of them do not know what farms, or what kinds of farms, or where the farms are, or what knowledge or skills are involved in farming. They apparently have little doubt that farms will continue to produce, but they do not know how or over what obstacles. For them, then, food is pretty much an abstract idea—something they do not know or imagine—until it appears on the grocery shelf or on the table.

The specialization of production induces specialization of consumption. Patrons of the entertainment industry, for example, entertain themselves less and less and have become more and more passively dependent on commercial suppliers. This is certainly true also of patrons of the food industry, who have tended more and more to be *mere* consumers—passive, uncritical, and dependent. Indeed, this sort of consumption may be said to be one of the chief goals of industrial production. The food industrialists have by now persuaded millions of consumers to prefer food that is already prepared. They will grow, deliver, and cook your food for you and (just like your mother) beg you to eat it. That they do not yet offer to insert it, prechewed, into your mouth is only because they have found no profitable way to do so. We may rest assured that they would be glad to find such a way. The ideal industrial food consumer would be strapped to a table with a tube running from the food factory directly into his or her stomach.

Perhaps I exaggerate, but not by much. The industrial eater is, in fact, one who does not know that eating is an agricultural act, who no longer knows or imagines the connections between eating and the land, and who is therefore necessarily passive and uncritical—in short, a victim. When food, in the minds of eaters, is no longer associated with farming and with the land, then the eaters are suffering a kind of cultural amnesia that is misleading and dangerous. The current version of the "dream home" of the future involves "effortless" shopping from a list of available goods on a television monitor and heating precooked food by remote control. Of course, this implies and depends on, a perfect ignorance of the history of the food that is consumed. It requires that the citizenry should give up their hereditary and sensible aversion to buying a pig in a poke. It wishes to make the selling of pigs in pokes an honorable and glamorous activity. The dreamer in this dream home will perforce know nothing about the kind or quality of this food, or where it came from, or how it was produced and prepared, or what ingredients, additives, and residues it contains—unless, that is, the dreamer undertakes a close and constant study of the food industry, in which case he or she might as well wake up and play an active and responsible part in the economy of food.

There is, then, a politics of food that, like any politics, involves our freedom. We still (sometimes) remember that we cannot be free if our minds and voices are controlled by someone else. But we have neglected to understand that we cannot be free if our food and its sources are controlled by someone else. The condition of the passive consumer of food is not a democratic condition. One reason to eat responsibly is to live free.

But if there is a food politics, there are also a food esthetics and a food ethics, neither of which is dissociated from politics. Like industrial sex, industrial eating has become a degraded, poor, and paltry thing. Our kitchens and other eating places more and more resemble filling stations, as our homes more and more resemble motels. "Life is not very interesting," we seem to have decided. "Let its satisfactions be minimal, perfunctory, and fast." We hurry through our meals to go to work and hurry through our work in order to "recreate" ourselves in the evenings and on weekends and vacations. And then we hurry, with the greatest possible speed and noise and violence, through our recreation—for what? To eat the billionth hamburger at some fast-food joint hellbent on increasing the "quality" of our life? And all this is carried out in a remarkable obliviousness to the causes and effects, the possibilities and the purposes, of the life of the body in this world.

One will find this obliviousness represented in virgin purity in the advertisements of the food industry, in which food wears as much makeup as the actors. If one gained one's whole knowledge of food from these advertisements (as some presumably do), one would not know that the various edibles were ever living creatures, or that they all come from the soil, or that they were produced by work. The passive American consumer, sitting down to a meal of pre-prepared or fast food, confronts a platter covered with inert, anonymous substances that have been processed, dyed, breaded, sauced, gravied, ground, pulped, strained, blended, prettified, and sanitized beyond resemblance to any part of any creature that ever lived. The products of nature and agriculture have been made, to all appearances, the products of industry. Both eater and eaten are thus in exile from biological reality. And the result is a kind of solitude, unprecedented in human experience, in which the eater may think of eating as, first, a purely commercial transaction between him and a supplier and then as a purely appetitive transaction between him and his food.

And this peculiar specialization of the act of eating is, again, of obvious benefit to the food industry, which has good reasons to obscure the connection between food and farming. It would not do for the consumer to know that the hamburger she is eating came from a steer who spent much of his life standing deep in his own excrement in a feedlot, helping to pollute the local streams, or that the calf that yielded the veal cutlet on her plate spent its life in a box in which it did not have room to turn around. And, though her sympathy for the slaw might be less tender, she should not be encouraged to meditate on the hygienic and biological implications of mile-square fields of cabbage, for vegetables grown in huge monocultures are dependent on toxic chemicals—just as animals in close confinement are dependent on antibiotics and other drugs.

The consumer, that is to say, must be kept from discovering that, in the food industry—as in any other industry—the overriding concerns are not quality and health, but volume and price. For decades now the entire industrial food economy, from the large farms and feedlots to the chains of supermarkets and fast-food restaurants, has been obsessed with volume. It has relentlessly increased scale in order to increase volume in order (presumably) to reduce costs. But as scale increases, diversity declines; as diversity declines, so does health; as health declines, the dependence on drugs and chemicals necessarily increases. As capital replaces labor, it does so by substituting machines, drugs, and chemicals for human workers and for the natural health and fertility of the soil. The food is produced by any means or any shortcut that will increase profits. And the business of the cosmeticians of advertising is to persuade the consumer that food so produced is good, tasty, healthful, and a guarantee of marital fidelity and long life.

It is possible, then, to be liberated from the husbandry and wifery of the old household food economy. But one can be thus liberated only by entering a trap (unless one sees ignorance and helplessness as the signs of privilege, as many people apparently do). The trap is the ideal of industrialism: a walled city surrounded by valves that let merchandise in but no consciousness out. How does one escape this trap? Only voluntarily, the same way that one went in: by restoring one's consciousness of what is involved in eating; by reclaiming responsibility for one's own part in the food economy. One might begin with the illuminating principle of Sir Albert Howard's *The Soil and Health*, that we should understand "the whole problem of health in soil, plant, animal, and man as one great subject." Eaters, that is, must understand that eating takes place inescapably in the world, that it is inescapably an agricultural act, and that how we eat determines, to a considerable extent, how the world is used. This is a simple way of describing a relationship that is inexpressibly complex. To eat responsibly is to understand and enact, so far as one can, this complex relationship. What can one do? Here is a list, probably not definitive:

1. Participate in food production to the extent that you can. If you have a yard or even just a porch box or a pot in a sunny window, grow something to eat in it. Make a little compost of your

kitchen scraps and use it for fertilizer. Only by growing some food for yourself can you become acquainted with the beautiful energy cycle that revolves from soil to seed to flower to fruit to food to offal to decay, and around again. You will be fully responsible for any food that you grow for yourself, and you will know all about it. You will appreciate it fully, having known it all its life.

2. Prepare your own food. This means reviving in your own mind and life the arts of kitchen and household. This should enable you to eat more cheaply, and it will give you a measure of "quality control": you will have some reliable knowledge of what has been added to the food you eat.

3. Learn the origins of the food you buy, and buy the food that is produced closest to your home. The idea that every locality should be, as much as possible, the source of its own food makes several kinds of sense. The locally produced food supply is the most secure, the freshest, and the easiest for local consumers to know about and to influence.

4. Whenever possible, deal directly with a local farmer, gardener, or orchardist. All the reasons listed for the previous suggestion apply here. In addition, by such dealing you eliminate the whole pack of merchants, transporters, processors, packagers, and advertisers who thrive at the expense of both producers and consumers.

5. Learn, in self-defense, as much as you can of the economy and technology of industrial food production. What is added to food that is not food, and what do you pay for these additions?

6. Learn what is involved in the *best* farming and gardening.

7. Learn as much as you can, by direct observation and experience if possible, of the life histories of the food species.

The last suggestion seems particularly important to me. Many people are now as much estranged from the lives of domestic plants and animals (except for flowers and dogs and cats) as they are from the lives of the wild ones. This is regrettable, for these domestic creatures are in diverse ways attractive; there is much pleasure in knowing them. And farming, animal husbandry, horticulture, and gardening, at their best, are complex and comely arts; there is much pleasure in knowing them, too.

It follows that there is great *dis*pleasure in knowing about a food economy that degrades and abuses those arts and those plants and animals and the soil from which they come. For anyone who does know something of the modern history of food, eating away from home can be a chore. My own inclination is to eat seafood instead of red meat or poultry when I am traveling. Though I am by no means a vegetarian, I dislike the thought that some animal has been made miserable in order to feed me. If I am going to eat meat, I want it to be from an animal that has lived a pleasant, uncrowded life outdoors, on bountiful pasture, with good water nearby and trees for shade. And I am getting almost as fussy about food plants. I like to eat vegetables and fruits that I know have lived happily and healthily in good soil, not the products of the huge, bechemicaled factory-fields that I have seen, for example, in the Central Valley of California. The industrial farm is said to have been patterned on the factory production line. In practice, it looks more like a concentration camp.

The pleasure of eating should be an *extensive* pleasure, not that of the mere gourmet. People who know the garden in which their vegetables have grown and know that the garden is healthy will remember the beauty of the growing plants, perhaps in the dewy first light of morning when gardens are at their best. Such a memory involves itself with the food and is one of the pleasures of eating. The knowledge of the good health of the garden relieves and frees and comforts the eater. The same goes for eating meat. The thought of the good pasture and of the calf contentedly grazing flavors the steak. Some, I know, will think it bloodthirsty or worse to eat a fellow creature you have known all its life. On the contrary, I think it means that you eat with understanding and with gratitude. A significant part of the pleasure of eating is in one's accurate consciousness of the lives and the world from which food comes. The pleasure of eating, then, may be the best available standard of our health. And this pleasure, I think, is pretty fully available to the urban consumer who will make the necessary effort.

I mentioned earlier the politics, esthetics, and ethics of food. But to speak of the pleasure of eating is to go beyond those categories. Eating with the fullest pleasure—pleasure, that is, that does not depend on ignorance—is perhaps the profoundest enactment of our connection with the world. In this pleasure we experience and celebrate our dependence and our gratitude, for we are living from mystery, from creatures we did not make and powers we cannot comprehend. When I think of the meaning of food, I always remember these lines by the poet William Carlos Williams, which seem to me merely honest:

> There is nothing to eat,
>   seek it where you will,
>   but the body of the Lord.
> The blessed plants
>   and the sea, yield it
>   to the imagination
> intact.

1989

THE WORK

OF LOCAL CULTURE

For many years, my walks have taken me down an old fencerow in a wooded hollow on what was once my grandfather's farm. A battered galvanized bucket is hanging on a fence post near the head of the hollow, and I never go by it without stopping to look inside. For what is going on in that bucket is the most momentous thing I know, the greatest miracle that I have ever heard of: it is making earth. The old bucket has hung there through many autumns, and the leaves have fallen around it and some have fallen into it. Rain and snow have fallen into it, and the fallen leaves have held the moisture and so have rotted. Nuts have fallen into it, or been carried into it by squirrels; mice and squirrels have eaten the meat of the nuts and left the shells; they and other animals have left their droppings; insects have flown into the bucket and died and decayed; birds have scratched in it and left their droppings or perhaps a feather or two. This slow work of growth and death, gravity and decay, which is the chief work of the world, has by now produced in the bottom of the bucket several inches of black humus. I look into that bucket with fascination because I am a farmer of sorts and an artist of sorts, and I recognize there an artistry and a farming far superior to mine, or to that of any human. I have seen the same process at work on the tops of boulders in a forest, and it has been at work immemorially over most of the land surface of the world. All creatures die into it, and they live by it.

The old bucket started out a far better one than you can buy now. I think it has been hanging on that post for something like fifty years. I think so because I remember hearing, when I was just a small boy, a story about a bucket that must have been this one. Several of my grandfather's black hired hands went out on an early spring day to burn a tobacco plant bed, and they took along some eggs to boil to eat with their dinner. When dinner time came and they looked around for something to boil the eggs in, they could find only an old bucket that at one time had been filled with tar. The boiling water softened the residue of tar, and one of the eggs came out of the water black. The hands made much sport of seeing who would have to eat the black egg, welcoming their laughter in the midst of their day's work. The man who had to eat the black egg was Floyd Scott, whom I remember well. Dry scales of tar still adhere to the inside of the bucket.

However small a landmark the old bucket is, it is not trivial. It is one of the signs by which I know my country and myself. And to me it is irresistibly suggestive in the way it collects leaves and other woodland sheddings as they fall through time. It collects stories, too, as they fall through time. It is irresistibly metaphorical. It is doing in a passive way what a human community must do actively and thoughtfully. A human community, too, must collect leaves and stories, and turn them to account. It must build soil, and build that memory of itself—in lore and story and song—that will be its culture. These two kinds of accumulation, of local soil and local culture, are intimately related.

In the woods, the bucket is no metaphor; it simply reveals what is always happening in the woods, if the woods is let alone. Of course, in most places in my part of the country, the human community did not leave the woods alone. It felled the trees and replaced them with pastures and crops. But this did not revoke the law of the woods, which is that the ground must be protected by a cover of vegetation and that the growth of the years must return—or be returned—to the ground to rot and build soil. A good local culture, in one of its most important functions, is a collection of the memories, ways, and skills necessary for the observance, within the bounds of domesticity, of this natural law. If the local culture cannot preserve and improve the local soil, then, as both reason and history inform us, the local community will decay and perish, and the work of soil building will be resumed by nature.

A human community, then, if it is to last long, must exert a sort of centripetal force, holding local soil and local memory in place. Practically speaking, human society has no work more important than this. Once we have acknowledged this principle, we can only be alarmed at the extent to which it has been ignored. For although our present society does generate a centripetal force of great power, this is not a local force, but one centered almost exclusively in our great commercial and industrial cities, which have drawn irresistibly into themselves both the products of the countryside and the people and talents of the country communities.

There is, as one assumes there must be, a countervailing or centrifugal force that also operates in our society, but this returns to the countryside not the residue of the land's growth to re-fertilize the fields, not the learning and experience of the greater world ready to go to work locally, and not—or not often—even a just monetary compensation. What are returned, instead, are overpriced manufactured goods, pollution in various forms, and garbage. A landfill on the edge of my own rural county in Kentucky, for example, daily receives about eighty truckloads of garbage. Fifty to sixty of these loads come from cities in New York, New Jersey, and Pennsylvania. Thus, the end result of the phenomenal modern productivity of the countryside is a debased countryside, which becomes daily less pleasant, and which will inevitably become less productive.

The cities, which have imposed this inversion of forces on the country, have been unable to preserve themselves from it. The typical modern city is surrounded by a circle of affluent suburbs, eating its way outward, like ringworm, leaving the so-called inner city desolate, filthy, ugly, and dangerous.

My walks in the hills and hollows around my home have inevitably produced in my mind the awareness that I live in a diminished country. The country has been and is being reduced by the great centralizing process that is our national economy. As I walk, I am always reminded of the slow, patient building of soil in the woods. And I am reminded of the events and companions of my life—for my walks, after so long, are cultural events. But under the trees and in the fields I see also the gullies and scars, healed or healing or fresh, left by careless logging and bad farming. I see the crumbling stone walls and the wire fences that have been rusting out ever since the 1930s. In the returning woods growth of the hollows, I see the sagging and the fallen barns, the empty and ruining houses, the houseless chimneys and foundations. As I look at this evidence of human life poorly founded, played out, and gone, I try to recover some understanding, some vision, of what this country was at the beginning: the great oaks and beeches and hickories, walnuts and maples, lindens and ashes, tulip poplars, standing in beauty and dignity now unimaginable, the black soil of their making, also no longer imaginable, lying deep at their feet—an incalculable birthright sold for money, most of which we did not receive. Most of the money made on the products of this place has gone to fill the pockets of people in distant cities who did not produce the products.

If my walks take me along the roads and streams, I see also the trash and the junk, carelessly manufactured and carelessly thrown away, the glass and the broken glass and the plastic and the aluminum that will lie here longer than the lifetime of trees— longer than the lifetime of our species, perhaps. And I know that this also is what we have to show for our participation in the American economy, for most of the money made on these things too has been made elsewhere.

It would be somewhat more pleasant for country people if they could blame all this on city people. But the old opposition of country versus city—though still true, and truer than ever economically, for the country is more than ever the colony of the city—is far too simple to explain our problem. For country people more and more live like city people, and so connive in their own ruin. More and more country people, like city people, allow their economic and social standards to be set by television and salesmen and outside experts. Our garbage mingles with New Jersey garbage in our local landfill, and it would be hard to tell which is which.

As local community decays along with local economy, a vast amnesia settles over the countryside. As the exposed and disregarded soil departs with the rains, so local knowledge and local memory move away to the cities or are forgotten under the influence of homogenized salestalk, entertainment, and education. This loss of local knowledge and local memory—that is, of local culture—has been ignored, or written off as one of the cheaper "prices of progress," or made the business of folklorists. Nevertheless, local culture has a value, and part of its value is economic. This can be demonstrated readily enough.

For example, when a community loses its memory, its members no longer know one another. How can they know one another if they have forgotten or have never learned one another's stories? If they do not know one another's stories, how can they know whether or not to trust one another? People who do not trust one another do not help one another, and moreover they fear one another. And this is our predicament now. Because of a general distrust and suspicion, we not only lose one another's help and companionship, but we are all now living in jeopardy of being sued.

We don't trust our "public servants" because we know that they don't respect us. They don't respect us, as we understand, because they don't know us; they don't know our stories. They expect us to sue them if they make mistakes, and so they must insure themselves, at great expense to them and to us. Doctors in a country community must send their patients to specialists in the city, not necessarily because they believe that they are wrong in their diagnoses, but because they know that they are not infallible and they must protect themselves against lawsuits, at great expense to us.

The government of my home county, which has a population of about ten thousand people, pays an annual liability insurance premium of about $34,000. Add to this the liability premiums that are paid by every professional person who is "at risk" in the county, and you get some idea of the load we are carrying. Several decent family livelihoods are annually paid out of the county to insurance companies for a service that is only negative and provisional.

All of this money is lost to us by the failure of community. A good community, as we know, insures itself by trust, by good faith and good will, by mutual help. A good community, in other words, is a good local economy. It depends on itself for many of its essential needs and is thus shaped, so to speak, from the inside—unlike most modern populations that depend on distant purchases for almost everything and are thus shaped from the outside by the purposes and the influence of salesmen.

I was walking one Sunday afternoon several years ago with an older friend. We went by the ruining log house that had belonged to his grandparents and great-grandparents. The house stirred my friend's memory, and he told how the oldtime people used to visit each other in the evenings, especially in the long evenings of winter. There used to be a sort of institution in our part of the country known as "sitting till bedtime." After supper, when they weren't too tired, neighbors would walk across the fields to visit each other. They popped corn, my friend said, and ate apples and talked. They told each other stories. They told each other stories, as I knew myself, that they all had heard before. Sometimes they told stories about each other, about themselves, living again in their own memories and thus keeping their memories alive. Among the hearers of these stories were always the children. When bedtime came, the visitors lit their lanterns and went home. My friend talked about this, and thought about it, and then he said, "They had everything but money."

They were poor, as country people have often been, but they had each other, they had their local economy in which they helped each other, they had each other's comfort when they needed it, and they had their stories, their history together in that place. To have everything but money is to have much. And most people of the present can only marvel to think of neighbors entertaining themselves for a whole evening without a single imported pleasure and without listening to a single minute of sales talk.

Most of the descendants of those people have now moved away, partly because of the cultural and economic failures that I mentioned earlier, and most of them no longer sit in the evenings and talk to anyone. Most of them now sit until bedtime watching TV, submitting every few minutes to a sales talk. The message of both the TV programs and the sales talks is that the watchers should spend whatever is necessary to be like everybody else.

By television and other public means, we are encouraged to believe that we are far advanced beyond sitting till bedtime with the neighbors on a Kentucky ridgetop, and indeed beyond anything we ever were before. But if, for example, there should occur a forty-eight-hour power failure, we would find ourselves in much more backward circumstances than our ancestors. What, for starters, would we do for entertainment? Tell each other stories? But most of us no longer talk with each other, much less tell each other stories. We tell our stories now mostly to doctors or lawyers or psychiatrists or insurance adjusters or the police, not to our neighbors for their (and our) entertainment. The stories that now entertain us are made up for us in New York or Los Angeles or other centers of such commerce.

But a forty-eight-hour power failure would involve almost unimaginable deprivations. It would be difficult to travel, especially in cities. Most of the essential work could not be done. Our windowless modern schools and other such buildings that depend on air conditioning could not be used. Refrigeration would be impossible; food would spoil. It would be difficult or impossible to prepare meals. If it was winter, heating systems would fail. At the end of forty-eight hours many of us would be hungry.

Such a calamity (and it is a modest one among those that our time has made possible) would thus reveal how far most of us are now living from our cultural and economic sources, and how extensively we have destroyed the foundations of local life. It would show us how far we have strayed from the locally centered life of such neighborhoods as the one my friend described—a life based to a considerable extent on what we now call solar energy, which is decentralized, democratic, clean, and free. If we note that much of the difference we are talking about can be accounted for as an increasing dependence on energy sources that are centralized, undemocratic, filthy, and expensive, we will have completed a sort of historical parable.

How has this happened? There are many reasons for it. One of the chief reasons is that everywhere in our country the local succession of the generations has been broken. We can trace this change through a series of stories that we may think of as cultural landmarks.

Throughout most of our literature, the normal thing was for the generations to succeed one another in place. The memorable stories occurred when this succession failed or became difficult or was somehow threatened. The norm is given in Psalm 128, in which this succession is seen as one of the rewards of righteousness: "Thou shalt see thy children's children, and peace upon Israel."

The longing for this result seems to have been universal. It presides also over *The Odyssey*, in which Odysseus's desire to return home is certainly regarded as normal. And this story is also much concerned with the psychology of family succession. Telemachus, Odysseus's son, comes of age in preparing for the return of his long-absent father; and it seems almost that Odysseus is enabled to return home by his son's achievement of enough manhood to go in search of him. Long after the return of both father and son, Odysseus's life will complete itself, as we know from Teiresias's prophecy in Book XI, much in the spirit of Psalm 128:

> A seaborne death
> soft as this hand of mist will come upon you
> when you are wearied out with sick old age,
> your country folk in blessed peace around you.

The Bible makes much of what it sees as the normal succession, in such stories as those of Abraham, Isaac, and Jacob, or of David and Solomon, in which the son completes the work or the destiny of the father. The parable of the prodigal son is prepared for by such Old Testament stories as that of Jacob, who errs, wanders, returns, is forgiven, and takes his place in the family lineage.

Shakespeare was concerned throughout his working life with the theme of the separation and rejoining of parents and children. It is there at the beginning in *The Comedy of Errors*, and he is still thinking about it when he gets to *King Lear* and *Pericles* and *The Tempest*. When Lear walks onstage with Cordelia dead in his arms, the theme of return is fulfilled, only this time in the way of tragedy.

Wordsworth's poem "Michael," written in 1800, is in the same line of descent. It is the story of a prodigal son, and return is still understood as the norm; before the boy's departure, he and his father make a "covenant" that he will return home and carry on his father's life as a shepherd on their ancestral pastures. But the ancient theme here has two significant differences: the son leaves home for an economic reason, and he does not return. Old Michael, the father, was long ago "bound / In surety for his brother's son." This nephew has failed in his business, and Michael is "summoned to discharge the forfeiture." Rather than do this by selling a portion of their patrimony, the aged parents decide that they must send their son to work for another kinsman in the city in order to earn the necessary money. The country people all are poor; there is no money to be earned at home. When the son has cleared the debt from the land, he will return to it to "possess it, free as the wind / That passes over it." But the son goes to the city, is corrupted by it, eventually commits a crime, and is forced "to seek a hiding place beyond the seas."

"Michael" is a sort of cultural watershed. It carries on the theme of return that goes back to the beginnings of Western culture, but that return now is only a desire and a memory; in the poem it fails to happen. Because of that failure, we see in "Michael" not just a local story of the Lake District of England, which it is, but the story of rural families in the industrial nations from Wordsworth's time until today. The children go to the cities, for reasons imposed by the external economy, and they do not return; eventually the parents die and the family land, like Michael's, is sold to a stranger. By now it has happened millions of times.

And by now the transformation of the ancient story is nearly complete. Our sociey, on the whole, has forgotten or repudiated the theme of return. Young people still grow up in rural families and go off to the cities, not to return. But now it is felt that this is what they *should* do. Now the norm is to leave and not return. And this applies as much to urban families as to rural ones. In the present urban economy the parent-child succession is possible only among the economically privileged. The children of industrial underlings are not likely to succeed their parents at work, and there is no reason for them to wish to do so. We are not going to have an industrial "Michael" in which it is perceived as tragic that a son fails to succeed his father on an assembly line.

According to the new norm, the child's destiny is not to succeed the parents, but to outmode them; succession has given way to supersession. And this norm is institutionalized not in great communal stories, but in the education system. The schools are no longer oriented to a cultural inheritance that it is their duty to pass on unimpaired, but to the career, which is to say the future, of the child. The orientation is thus necessarily theoretical, speculative, and mercenary. The child is not educated to return home and be of use to the place and community; he or she is educated to *leave* home and earn money in a provisional future that has nothing to do with place or community. And parents with children in school are likely to find themselves immediately separated from their children, and made useless to them, by the intervention of new educational techniques, technologies, methods, and languages. School systems innovate as compulsively and as eagerly as factories. It is no wonder that, under these circumstances, "educators" tend to look upon the parents as a bad influence and wish to take the children away from home as early as possible. And many parents, in truth, are now finding their children an encumbrance at home, where there is no useful work for them to do, and are glad enough to turn them over to the state for the use of the future. The extent to which this order of things is now dominant is suggested by a recent magazine article on the discovery of what purports to be a new idea:

> The idea that a parent can be a teacher at home has caught the attention of educators. . . . Parents don't have to be graduates of Harvard or Yale to help their kids learn and achieve.*

Thus the home as a place where a child can learn becomes an *idea* of the professional "educator," who retains control of the idea. The home, as the article makes clear, is not to be a place where children may learn on their own, but a place where they are taught by parents according to the instructions of professional "educators." In fact, the Home and School Institute, Inc., of Washington, D.C. (known, of course, as "the HSI") has been "founded to show . . . how to involve families in their kids' educations."

In such ways as this, the nuclei of home and community have been invaded by the organizations, just as have the nuclei of cells

*Marianne Merrill Moates, "Learning . . . Every Day," *Creative Ideas for Living*, July/August 1988, p. 89.

and atoms. And we must be careful to see that the old cultural centers of home and community were made vulnerable to this invasion by their failure as economies. If there is no household or community economy, then family members and neighbors are no longer useful to one another. When people are no longer useful to one another, then the centripetal force of family and community fails, and people fall into dependence on exterior economies and organizations. The hegemony of professionals and professionalism erects itself on local failure, and from then on the locality exists merely as a market for consumer goods and as a source of "raw material," human and natural. The local schools no longer serve the local community; they serve the government's economy and the economy's government. Unlike the local community, the government and the economy cannot be served with affection, but only with professional zeal or professional boredom. Professionalism means more interest in salaries and less interest in what used to be known as disciplines. And so we arrive at the idea, endlessly reiterated in the news media, that education can be improved by bigger salaries for teachers— which may be true, but education cannot be improved, as the proponents too often imply, by bigger salaries alone. There must also be love of learning and of the cultural tradition and of excellence—and this love cannot exist, because it makes no sense, apart from the love of a place and a community. Without this love, education is only the importation into a local community of centrally prescribed "career preparation" designed to facilitate the export of young careerists.

Our children are educated, then, to leave home, not to stay home, and the costs of this education have been far too little acknowledged. One of the costs is psychological, and the other is at once cultural and ecological.

The natural or normal course of human growing up must begin with some sort of rebellion against one's parents, for it is clearly impossible to grow up if one remains a child. But the child, in the process of rebellion and of achieving the emotional and economic independence that rebellion ought to lead to, finally comes to understand the parents as fellow humans and fellow sufferers, and in some manner returns to them as their friend, forgiven and forgiving the inevitable wrongs of family life. That is the old norm.

The new norm, according to which the child leaves home as a student and never lives at home again, interrupts the old course of coming of age at the point of rebellion, so that the child is apt to remain stalled in adolescence, never achieving any kind of reconciliation or friendship with the parents. Of course, such a return and reconciliation cannot be achieved without the recognition of mutual practical need. In the present economy, however, where individual dependences are so much exterior to both household and community, family members often have no practical need or use for one another. Hence the frequent futility of attempts at a purely psychological or emotional reconciliation.

And this interposition of rebellion and then of geographical and occupational distance between parents and children may account for the peculiar emotional intensity that our society attaches to innovation. We appear to hate whatever went before, very much as an adolescent hates parental rule, and to look on its obsolescence as a kind of vengeance. Thus we may explain industry's obsessive emphasis on "this year's model," or the preoccupation of the professional "educators" with theoretical and methodological innovation. Similarly, in modern literature we have had for many years an emphasis on "originality" and "the anxiety of influence" (an adolescent critical theory), as opposed, say, to Spenser's filial admiration for Chaucer, or Dante's for Virgil.

But if the new norm interrupts the development of the relation between children and parents, that same interruption, ramifying through a community, destroys the continuity and so the integrity of local life. As the children depart, generation after generation, the place loses its memory of itself, which is its history and its culture. And the local history, if it survives at all, loses its place. It does no good for historians, folklorists, and anthropologists to collect the songs and the stories and the lore that make up local culture and store them in books and archives. They cannot collect and store—because they cannot know—the pattern of reminding that can survive only in the living human community in its place. It is this pattern that is the life of local culture and that brings it usefully or pleasurably to mind. Apart from its local landmarks and occasions, the local culture may be the subject of curiosity or of study, but it is also dead.

The loss of local culture is, in part, a practical loss and an economic one. For one thing, such a culture contains, and conveys to succeeding generations, the history of the use of the place and the knowledge of how the place may be lived in and used. For another, the pattern of reminding implies affection for the place and respect for it, and so, finally, the local culture will carry the knowledge of how the place may be well and lovingly used, and also the implicit command to use it *only* well and lovingly. The only true and effective "operator's manual for spaceship earth" is not a book that any human will ever write; it is hundreds of thousands of local cultures.

Lacking an authentic local culture, a place is open to exploitation, and ultimately destruction, from the center. Recently, for example, I heard the dean of a prominent college of agriculture interviewed on the radio. What have we learned, he was asked, from last summer's drouth? And he replied that "we" need to breed more drouth resistance into plants, and that "we" need a government "safety net" for farmers. He might have said that farmers need to re-examine their farms and their circumstances in light of the drouth, and to think again on such subjects as diversification, scale, and the mutual helpfulness of neighbors. But he did not say that. To him, the drouth was merely an opportunity for agribusiness corporations and the government, by which the farmers and rural communities could only become more dependent on the economy that is destroying them. This is as good an example as any of the centralized thinking of a centralized economy—to which the only effective answer that I know is a strong local community with a strong local economy and a strong local culture.

For a long time now, the prevailing assumption has been that if the nation is all right, then all the localities within it will be all right also. I see little reason to believe that this is true. At present, in fact, both the nation and the national economy are living at the expense of localities and local communities—as all small-town and country people have reason to know. In rural America, which is in many ways a colony of what the government and the corporations think of as the nation, most of us have experienced the losses that I have been talking about: the departure of young people, of soil and other so-called natural resources, and of local memory. We feel ourselves crowded more and more into a dimensionless present, in which the past is forgotten and the future, even in our most optimistic "projections," is forbidding and fearful. Who can desire a future that is determined entirely by the purposes of the most wealthy and the most powerful, and by the capacities of machines?

Two questions, then, remain: Is a change for the better possible? And who has the power to make such a change? I still believe that a change for the better is possible, but I confess that my belief is partly hope and partly faith. No one who hopes for improvement should fail to see and respect the signs that we may be approaching some sort of historical waterfall, past which we will not, by changing our minds, be able to change anything else. We know that at any time an ecological or a technological or a political event that we will have allowed may remove from us the power to make change and leave us with the mere necessity to submit to it. Beyond that, the two questions are one: the possibility of change depends on the existence of people who have the power to change.

Does this power reside at present in the national government? That seems to me extremely doubtful. To anyone who has read the papers during the recent presidential campaign, it must be clear that at the highest level of government there is, properly speaking, no political discussion. Are the corporations likely to help us? We know, from long experience, that the corporations will assume no responsibility that is not forcibly imposed upon them by government. The record of the corporations is written too plainly in verifiable damage to permit us to expect much from them. May we look for help to the universities? Well, the universities are more and more the servants of government and the corporations.

Most urban people evidently assume that all is well. They live too far from the exploited and endangered sources of their economy to need to assume otherwise. Some urban people are becoming disturbed about the contamination of air, water, and food, and that is promising, but there are not enough of them yet to make much difference. There is enough trouble in the "inner cities" to make them likely places of change, and evidently change is in them, but it is desperate and destructive change. As if to perfect their exploitation by other people, the people of the "inner cities" are destroying both themselves and their places.

My feeling is that if improvement is going to begin anywhere, it will have to begin out in the country and in the country towns. This is not because of any intrinsic virtue that can be ascribed to rural people, but because of their circumstances. Rural people are living, and have lived for a long time, at the site of the trouble. They see all around them, every day, the marks and scars of an exploitive national economy. They have much reason, by now, to know how little real help is to be expected from somewhere else. They still have, moreover, the remnants of local memory and local community. And in rural communities there are still farms and small businesses that can be changed according to the will and the desire of individual people.

In this difficult time of failed public expectations, when thoughtful people wonder where to look for hope, I keep returning in my own mind to the thought of the renewal of the rural communities. I know that one revived rural community would be more convincing and more encouraging than all the government and university programs of the last fifty years, and I think that it could be the beginning of the renewal of our country, for the renewal of rural communities ultimately implies the renewal of urban ones. But to be authentic, a true encouragement and a true beginning, this would have to be a revival accomplished mainly by the community itself. It would have to be done not from the outside by the instruction of visiting experts, but from the inside by the ancient rule of neighborliness, by the love of precious things, and by the wish to be at home.

1988

WHY I AM NOT GOING
TO BUY A COMPUTER

Like almost everybody else, I am hooked to the energy corporations, which I do not admire. I hope to become less hooked to them. In my work, I try to be as little hooked to them as possible. As a farmer, I do almost all of my work with horses. As a writer, I work with a pencil or a pen and a piece of paper.

My wife types my work on a Royal standard typewriter bought new in 1956 and as good now as it was then. As she types, she sees things that are wrong and marks them with small checks in the margins. She is my best critic because she is the one most familiar with my habitual errors and weaknesses. She also understands, sometimes better than I do, what *ought* to be said. We have, I think, a literary cottage industry that works well and pleasantly. I do not see anything wrong with it.

A number of people, by now, have told me that I could greatly improve things by buying a computer. My answer is that I am not going to do it. I have several reasons, and they are good ones.

The first is the one I mentioned at the beginning. I would hate to think that my work as a writer could not be done without a direct dependence on strip-mined coal. How could I write conscientiously against the rape of nature if I were, in the act of writing, implicated in the rape? For the same reason, it matters to me that my writing is done in the daytime, without electric light.

I do not admire the computer manufacturers a great deal more than I admire the energy industries. I have seen their advertisements, attempting to seduce struggling or failing farmers into the belief that they can solve their problems by buying yet another piece of expensive equipment. I am familiar with their propaganda campaigns that have put computers into public schools in need of books. That computers are expected to become as common as TV sets in "the future" does not impress me or matter to me. I do not own a TV set. I do not see that computers are bringing us one step nearer to anything that does matter to me: peace, economic justice, ecological health, political honesty, family and community stability, good work.

What would a computer cost me? More money, for one thing, than I can afford, and more than I wish to pay to people whom I do not admire. But the cost would not be just monetary. It is well understood that technological innovation always requires the discarding of the "old model"—the "old model" in this case being not just our old Royal standard, but my wife, my critic, my closest reader, my fellow worker. Thus (and I think this is typical of present-day technological innovation), what would be superseded would be not only something, but somebody. In order to be technologically up-to-date as a writer, I would have to sacrifice an association that I am dependent upon and that I treasure.

My final and perhaps my best reason for not owning a computer is that I do not wish to fool myself. I disbelieve, and therefore strongly resent, the assertion that I or anybody else could write better or more easily with a computer than with a pencil. I do not see why I should not be as scientific about this as the next fellow: when somebody has used a computer to write work that is demonstrably better than Dante's, and when this better is demonstrably attributable to the use of a computer, then I will speak of computers with a more respectful tone of voice, though I still will not buy one.

To make myself as plain as I can, I should give my standards for technological innovation in my own work. They are as follows:

1. The new tool should be cheaper than the one it replaces.

2. It should be at least as small in scale as the one it replaces.

3. It should do work that is clearly and demonstrably better than the one it replaces.

4. It should use less energy than the one it replaces.

5. If possible, it should use some form of solar energy, such as that of the body.

6. It should be repairable by a person of ordinary intelligence, provided that he or she has the necessary tools.

7. It should be purchasable and repairable as near to home as possible.

8. It should come from a small, privately owned shop or store that will take it back for maintenance and repair.

9. It should not replace or disrupt anything good that already exists, and this includes family and community relationships.

1987

After the foregoing essay, first published in the *New England Review and Bread Loaf Quarterly*, was reprinted in *Harper's*, the *Harper's* editors published the following letters in response and permitted me a reply.   w. b.

LETTERS

Wendell Berry provides writers enslaved by the computer with a handy alternative: Wife—a low-tech energy-saving device. Drop a pile of handwritten notes on Wife and you get back a finished manuscript, edited while it was typed. What computer can do that? Wife meets all of Berry's uncompromising standards for technological innovation: she's cheap, repairable near home, and good for the family structure. Best of all, Wife is politically correct because she breaks a writer's "direct dependence on strip-mined coal."

History teaches us that Wife can also be used to beat rugs

and wash clothes by hand, thus eliminating the need for the vacuum cleaner and washing machine, two more nasty machines that threaten the act of writing.

Gordon Inkeles
Miranda, Calif.

I have no quarrel with Berry because he prefers to write with pencil and paper; that is his choice. But he implies that I and others are somehow impure because we choose to write on a computer. I do not admire the energy corporations, either. Their shortcoming is not that they produce electricity but how they go about it. They are poorly managed because they are blind to long-term consequences. To solve this problem, wouldn't it make more sense to correct the precise error they are making rather than simply ignore their product? I would be happy to join Berry in a protest against strip mining, but I intend to keep plugging this computer into the wall with a clear conscience.

James Rhoads
Battle Creek, Mich.

I enjoyed reading Berry's declaration of intent never to buy a personal computer in the same way that I enjoy reading about the belief systems of unfamiliar tribal cultures. I tried to imagine a tool that would meet Berry's criteria for superiority to his old manual typewriter. The clear winner is the quill pen. It is cheaper, smaller, more energy-efficient, human-powered, easily repaired, and non-disruptive of existing relationships.

Berry also requires that this tool must be "clearly and demonstrably better" than the one it replaces. But surely we all recognize by now that "better" is in the mind of the beholder. To the quill pen aficionado, the benefits obtained from elegant calligraphy might well outweigh all others.

I have no particular desire to see Berry use a word processor; if he doesn't like computers, that's fine with me. However, I do object to his portrayal of this reluctance as a moral virtue. Many of us have found that computers can be an invaluable tool in the fight to protect our environment. In addition to helping me write, my personal computer gives me access to up-to-the-minute reports on the workings of the EPA and the nuclear industry. I participate in electronic bulletin boards on which environmental activists discuss strategy and warn each other about urgent legislative issues. Perhaps Berry feels that the Sierra Club should eschew modern printing technology, which is highly wasteful of energy, in favor of having its members hand-copy the club's magazines and other mailings each month?

> *Nathaniel S. Borenstein*
> Pittsburgh, Pa.

The value of a computer to a writer is that it is a tool not for generating ideas but for typing and editing words. It is cheaper than a secretary (or a wife!) and arguably more fuel-efficient. And it enables spouses who are not inclined to provide free labor more time to concentrate on *their* own work.

We should support alternatives both to coal-generated electricity and to IBM-style technocracy. But I am reluctant to entertain alternatives that presuppose the traditional subservience of one class to another. Let the PCs come and the wives and servants go seek more meaningful work.

> *Toby Koosman*
> Knoxville, Tenn.

Berry asks how he could write conscientiously against the rape of nature if in the act of writing on a computer he was implicated in the rape. I find it ironic that a writer who sees the underlying connectedness of things would allow his diatribe against computers to be published in a magazine that carries ads for the National Rural Electric Cooperative Association, Marlboro, Phillips Petroleum, McDonnell Douglas, and yes, even Smith-Corona. If Berry rests comfortably at night, he must be using sleeping pills.

Bradley C. Johnson
Grand Forks, N.D.

WENDELL BERRY REPLIES:

The foregoing letters surprised me with the intensity of the feelings they expressed. According to the writers' testimony, there is nothing wrong with their computers; they are utterly satisfied with them and all that they stand for. My correspondents are certain that I am wrong and that I am, moreover, on the losing side, a side already relegated to the dustbin of history. And yet they grow huffy and condescending over my tiny dissent. What are they so anxious about?

I can only conclude that I have scratched the skin of a technological fundamentalism that, like other fundamentalisms, wishes to monopolize a whole society and, therefore, cannot tolerate the smallest difference of opinion. At the slightest hint of a threat to their complacency, they repeat, like a chorus of toads, the notes sounded by their leaders in industry. The past was gloomy, drudgery-ridden, servile, meaningless, and slow. The present, thanks only to purchasable products, is meaningful, bright, lively, centralized, and fast. The future, thanks only to more purchasable products, is going to be even better. Thus consumers become salesmen, and the world is made safer for corporations.

I am also surprised by the meanness with which two of these writers refer to my wife. In order to imply that I am a tyrant, they suggest by both direct statement and innuendo that she is subservient, characterless, and stupid—a mere "device" easily forced to provide meaningless "free labor." I understand that it is impossible to make an adequate public defense of one's private life, and so I will only point out that there are a number of kinder possibilities that my critics have disdained to imagine: that my wife may do this work because she wants to and likes to; that she may find some use and some meaning in it; that she may not work for nothing. These gentlemen obviously think themselves feminists of the most correct and principled sort, and yet they do not hesitate to stereotype and insult, on the basis of one fact, a woman they do not know. They are audacious and irresponsible gossips.

In his letter, Bradley C. Johnson rushes past the possibility of sense in what I said in my essay by implying that I am or ought to be a fanatic. That I am a person of this century and am implicated in many practices that I regret is fully acknowledged at the beginning of my essay. I did not say that I proposed to end forthwith all my involvement in harmful technology, for I do not know how to do that. I said merely that I want to limit such involvement, and to a certain extent I do know how to do that. If some technology does damage to the world—as two of the above letters seem to agree that it does—then why is it not reasonable, and indeed moral, to try to limit one's use of that technology? *Of course*, I think that I am right to do this.

I would not think so, obviously, if I agreed with Nathaniel S. Borenstein that " 'better' is in the mind of the beholder." But if he truly believes this, I do not see why he bothers with his personal computer's "up-to-the-minute reports on the workings of the EPA and the nuclear industry" or why he wishes to be warned about "urgent legislative issues." According to his system, the "better" in a bureaucratic, industrial, or legislative mind is as good as the "better" in his. His mind apparently is being subverted by an objective standard of some sort, and he had better look out.

Borenstein does not say what he does after his computer has drummed him awake. I assume from his letter that he must send donations to conservation organizations and letters to officials. Like James Rhoads, at any rate, he has a clear conscience. But this is what is wrong with the conservation movement. It has a clear conscience. The guilty are always other people, and the wrong is always somewhere else. That is why Borenstein finds his "electronic bulletin board" so handy. To the conservation movement, it is only production that causes environmental degradation; the consumption that supports the production is rarely acknowledged to be at fault. The ideal of the run-of-the-mill conservationist is to impose restraints upon production without limiting consumption or burdening the consciences of consumers.

But virtually all of our consumption now is extravagant, and virtually all of it consumes the world. It is not beside the point that most electrical power comes from strip-mined coal. The history of the exploitation of the Appalachian coal fields is long, and it is available to readers. I do not see how anyone can read it and plug in any appliance with a clear conscience. If Rhoads can do so, that does not mean that his conscience is clear; it means that his conscience is not working.

To the extent that we consume, in our present circumstances, we are guilty. To the extent that we guilty consumers are conservationists, we are absurd. But what can we do? Must we go on writing letters to politicians and donating to conservation organizations until the majority of our fellow citizens agree with us? Or can we do something directly to solve our share of the problem?

I am a conservationist. I believe wholeheartedly in putting pressure on the politicians and in maintaining the conservation organizations. But I wrote my little essay partly in distrust of centralization. I don't think that the government and the conservation organizations alone will ever make us a conserving society. Why do I need a centralized computer system to alert me to environmental crises? That I live every hour of every day in an environmental crisis I know from all my senses. Why then is not my first duty to reduce, so far as I can, my own consumption?

Finally, it seems to me that none of my correspondents recognizes the innovativeness of my essay. If the use of a computer is a new idea, then a newer idea is not to use one.

FEMINISM, THE BODY,
AND THE MACHINE

Some time ago *Harper's* reprinted a short essay of mine in which I gave some of my reasons for refusing to buy a computer. Until that time, the vast numbers of people who disagree with my writings had mostly ignored them. An unusual number of people, however, neglected to ignore my insensitivity to the wonders of computer enhancement. Some of us, it seems, would be better off if we would just realize that this is already the best of all possible worlds, and is going to get even better if we will just buy the right equipment.

Harper's published only five of the letters the editors received in response to my essay, and they published only negative letters. But of the twenty letters received by the *Harper's* editors, who forwarded copies to me, three were favorable. This I look upon as extremely gratifying. If these letters may be taken as a fair sample, then one in seven of *Harper's* readers agreed with me. If I had guessed beforehand, I would have guessed that my supporters would have been fewer than one in a thousand. And so I suppose, after further reflection, that my surprise at the intensity of the attacks on me is mistaken. There are more of us than I thought. Maybe there is even a "significant number" of us.

Only one of the negative letters seemed to me to have much intelligence in it. That one was from R. N. Neff of Arlington, Virginia, who scored a direct hit: "Not to be obtuse, but being willing to bare my illiterate soul for all to see, is there indeed a 'work demonstrably better than Dante's' . . . which was written on a Royal standard typewriter?" I like this retort so well that I am tempted to count it a favorable response, raising the total to four. The rest of the negative replies, like the five published ones, were more feeling than intelligent. Some of them, indeed, might be fairly described as exclamatory.

One of the letter writers described me as "a fool" and "doubly a fool," but fortunately misspelled my name, leaving me a speck of hope that I am not the "Wendell Barry" he was talking about. Two others accused me of self-righteousness, by which they seem to have meant that they think they are righter than I think I am. And another accused me of being more concerned about my own moral purity than with "any ecological effect," thereby making the sort of razor-sharp philosophical distinction that could cause a person to be elected president.

But most of my attackers deal in feelings either feminist or technological, or both. The feelings expressed seem to be representative of what the state of public feeling currently permits to be felt, and of what public rhetoric currently permits to be said. The feelings, that is, are similar enough, from one letter to another, to be thought representative, and as representative letters they have an interest greater than the quarrel that occasioned them.

Without exception, the feminist letters accuse me of exploiting my wife, and they do not scruple to allow the most insulting implications of their indictment to fall upon my wife. They fail entirely to see that my essay does not give any support to their accusation—or if they see it, they do not care. My essay, in fact, does not characterize my wife beyond saying that she types my manuscripts and tells me what she thinks about them. It does not say what her motives are, how much work she does, or whether or how she is paid. Aside from saying that she is my wife and that I value the help she gives me with my work, it says nothing about our marriage. It says nothing about our economy.

There is no way, then, to escape the conclusion that my wife and I are subjected in these letters to a condemnation by category. My offense is that I am a man who receives some help from his wife; my wife's offense is that she is a woman who does some work for her husband—which work, according to her critics and mine, makes her a drudge, exploited by a conventional subservience. And my detractors have, as I say, no evidence to support any of this. Their accusation rests on a syllogism of the flimsiest sort: my wife helps me in my work, some wives who have helped their husbands in their work have been exploited, therefore my wife is exploited.

This, of course, outrages justice to about the same extent that it insults intelligence. Any respectable system of justice exists in part as a protection against such accusations. In a just society nobody is expected to plead guilty to a general indictment, because in a just society nobody can be convicted on a general indictment. What is required for a just conviction is a particular accusation that can be *proved*. My accusers have made no such accusation against me.

That feminists or any other advocates of human liberty and dignity should resort to insult and injustice is regrettable. It is equally regrettable that all of the feminist attacks on my essay implicitly deny the validity of two decent and probably necessary possibilities: marriage as a state of mutual help, and the household as an economy.

Marriage, in what is evidently its most popular version, is now on the one hand an intimate "relationship" involving (ideally) two successful careerists in the same bed, and on the other hand a sort of private political system in which rights and interests must be constantly asserted and defended. Marriage, in other words, has now taken the form of divorce: a prolonged and impassioned negotiation as to how things shall be divided. During their understandably temporary association, the "married" couple will typically consume a large quantity of merchandise and a large portion of each other.

The modern household is the place where the consumptive couple do their consuming. Nothing productive is done there. Such work as is done there is done at the expense of the resident couple or family, and to the profit of suppliers of energy and household technology. For entertainment, the inmates consume television or purchase other consumable diversion elsewhere.

There are, however, still some married couples who understand themselves as belonging to their marriage, to each other, and to their children. What they have they have in common, and so, to them, helping each other does not seem merely to damage their ability to compete against each other. To them, "mine" is not so powerful or necessary a pronoun as "ours."

This sort of marriage usually has at its heart a household that is to some extent productive. The couple, that is, makes around itself a household economy that involves the work of both wife and husband, that gives them a measure of economic independence and self-protection, a measure of self-employment, a measure of freedom, as well as a common ground and a common satisfaction. Such a household economy may employ the disciplines and skills of housewifery, of carpentry and other trades of building and maintenance, of gardening and other branches of subsistence agriculture, and even of woodlot management and woodcutting. It may also involve a "cottage industry" of some kind, such as a small literary enterprise.

It is obvious how much skill and industry either partner may put into such a household and what a good economic result such work may have, and yet it is a kind of work now frequently held in contempt. Men in general were the first to hold it in contempt as they departed from it for the sake of the professional salary or the hourly wage, and now it is held in contempt by such feminists as those who attacked my essay. Thus farm wives who help to run the kind of household economy that I have described are apt to be asked by feminists, and with great condescension, "But what do you *do*?" By this they invariably mean that there is something better to do than to make one's marriage and household, and by better they invariably mean "employment outside the home."

I know that I am in dangerous territory, and so I had better be plain: what I have to say about marriage and household I mean to apply to men as much as to women. I do not believe that there is anything better to do than to make one's marriage and household, whether one is a man or a woman. I do not believe that "employment outside the home" is as valuable or important or satisfying as employment at home, for either men or women. It is clear to me from my experience as a teacher, for example, that children need an ordinary daily association with *both* parents. They need to see their parents at work; they need, at first, to play at the work they see their parents doing, and then they need to work with their parents. It does not matter so much that this working together should be what is called "quality time," but it matters a great deal that the work done should have the dignity of economic value.

I should say too that I understand how fortunate I have been in being able to do an appreciable part of my work at home. I know that in many marriages both husband and wife are now finding it necessary to work away from home. This issue, of course, is troubled by the question of what is meant by "necessary," but it is true that a family living that not so long ago was ordinarily supplied by one job now routinely requires two or more. My interest is not to quarrel with individuals, men or women, who work away from home, but rather to ask why we should consider this general working away from home to be a desirable state of things, either for people or for marriage, for our society or for our country.

If I had written in my essay that my wife worked as a typist and editor for a publisher, doing the same work that she does for me, no feminists, I daresay, would have written to *Harper's* to attack me for exploiting her—even though, for all they knew, I might have forced her to do such work in order to keep me in gambling money. It would have been assumed as a matter of course that if she had a job away from home she was a "liberated woman," possessed of a dignity that no home could confer upon her.

As I have said before, I understand that one cannot construct an adequate public defense of a private life. Anything that I might say here about my marriage would be immediately (and rightly) suspect on the ground that it would be only *my* testimony. But for the sake of argument, let us suppose that whatever work my wife does, as a member of our marriage and household, she does both as a full economic partner and as her own boss, and let us suppose that the economy we have is adequate to our needs. Why, granting that supposition, should anyone assume that my wife would increase her freedom or dignity or satisfaction by becoming the employee of a boss, who would be in turn also a corporate underling and in no sense a partner?

Why would any woman who would refuse, properly, to take the marital vow of obedience (on the ground, presumably, that subservience to a mere human being is beneath human dignity) then regard as "liberating" a job that puts her under the authority of a boss (man or woman) whose authority specifically requires and expects obedience? It is easy enough to see why women came to object to the role of Blondie, a mostly decorative custodian of a degraded, consumptive modern household, preoccupied with clothes, shopping, gossip, and outwitting her husband. But are we to assume that one may fittingly cease to be Blondie by becoming Dagwood? Is the life of a corporate underling—even acknowledging that corporate underlings are well paid—an acceptable end to our quest for human dignity and worth? It is clear enough by now that one does not cease to be an underling by reaching "the top." Corporate life is composed only of lower underlings and higher underlings. Bosses are everywhere, and all the bosses are underlings. This is invariably revealed when the time comes for accepting responsibility for something unpleasant, such as the Exxon fiasco in Prince William Sound, for which certain lower underlings are blamed but no higher underling is responsible. The underlings at the top, like telephone operators, have authority and power, but no responsibility.

And the oppressiveness of some of this office work defies belief. Edward Mendelson (in the *New Republic*, February 22,
1988) speaks of "the office worker whose computer keystrokes
are monitored by the central computer in the personnel office,
and who will be fired if the keystrokes-per-minute figure doesn't
match the corporate quota." (Mr. Mendelson does not say what
form of drudgery this worker is being saved from.) And what are
we to say of the diversely skilled country housewife who now
bores the same six holes day after day on an assembly line? What
higher form of womanhood or humanity is she evolving toward?

How, I am asking, can women improve themselves by submitting to the same specialization, degradation, trivialization,
and tyrannization of work that men have submitted to? And that
question is made legitimate by another: How have men improved themselves by submitting to it? The answer is that men
have not, and women cannot, improve themselves by submitting
to it.

Women have complained, justly, about the behavior of
"macho" men. But despite their he-man pretensions and their
captivation by masculine heroes of sports, war, and the Old
West, most men are now entirely accustomed to obeying and
currying the favor of their bosses. Because of this, of course, they
hate their jobs—they mutter, "Thank God it's Friday" and
"Pretty good for Monday"—but they do as they are told. They
are more compliant than most housewives have been. Their
characters combine feudal submissiveness with modern helplessness. They have accepted almost without protest, and often
with relief, their dispossession of any usable property and, with
that, their loss of economic independence and their consequent
subordination to bosses. They have submitted to the destruction
of the household economy and thus of the household, to the loss
of home employment and self-employment, to the disintegration
of their families and communities, to the desecration and pillage
of their country, and they have continued abjectly to believe,
obey, and vote for the people who have most eagerly abetted this

ruin and who have most profited from it. These men, moreover, are helpless to do anything for themselves or anyone else without money, and so for money they do whatever they are told. They know that their ability to be useful is precisely defined by their willingness to be somebody else's tool. Is it any wonder that they talk tough and worship athletes and cowboys? Is it any wonder that some of them are violent?

It is clear that women cannot justly be excluded from the daily fracas by which the industrial economy divides the spoils of society and nature, but their inclusion is a poor justice and no reason for applause. The enterprise is as devastating with women in it as it was before. There is no sign that women are exerting a "civilizing influence" upon it. To have an equal part in our juggernaut of national vandalism is to be a vandal. To call this vandalism "liberation" is to prolong, and even ratify, a dangerous confusion that was once principally masculine.

A broader, deeper criticism is necessary. The problem is not just the exploitation of women by men. A greater problem is that women and men alike are consenting to an economy that exploits women and men and everything else.

Another decent possibility my critics implicitly deny is that of work as a gift. Not one of them supposed that my wife may be a consulting engineer who helps me in her spare time out of the goodness of her heart; instead they suppose that she is "a household drudge." But what appears to infuriate them the most is their supposition that she works for nothing. They assume— and this is the orthodox assumption of the industrial economy— that the only help worth giving is not given at all, but sold. Love, friendship, neighborliness, compassion, duty—what are they? We are realists. We will be most happy to receive your check.

The various reductions I have been describing are fairly directly the results of the ongoing revolution of applied science known as "technological progress." This revolution has provided the means by which both the productive and the consumptive capacities of people could be detached from household and community and made to serve other people's purely economic ends. It has provided as well a glamor of newness, ease, and affluence that made it seductive even to those who suffered most from it. In its more recent history especially, this revolution has been successful in putting unheard-of quantities of consumer goods and services within the reach of ordinary people. But the technical means of this popular "affluence" has at the same time made possible the gathering of the real property and the real power of the country into fewer and fewer hands.

Some people would like to think that this long sequence of industrial innovations has changed human life and even human nature in fundamental ways. Perhaps it has—but, arguably, almost always for the worse. I know that "technological progress" can be defended, but I observe that the defenses are invariably quantitative—catalogs of statistics on the ownership of automobiles and television sets, for example, or on the increase of life expectancy—and I see that these statistics are always kept carefully apart from the related statistics of soil loss, pollution, social disintegration, and so forth. That is to say, there is never an effort to determine the *net* result of this progress. The voice of its defenders is not that of the responsible bookkeeper, but that of the propagandist or salesman, who says that the net gain is more than 100 percent—that the thing we have bought has perfectly replaced everything it has cost, and added a great deal more: "You just can't lose!" We thus have got rich by spending, just as the advertisers have told us we would, and the best of all possible worlds is getting better every day.

The statistics of life expectancy are favorites of the industrial apologists, because they are perhaps the hardest to argue with. Nevertheless, this emphasis on longevity is an excellent example of the way the isolated aims of the industrial mind reduce and distort human life, and also the way statistics corrupt the truth. A long life has indeed always been thought desirable; everything that is alive apparently wishes to continue to live. But until our own time, that sentence would have been qualified: long life is desirable and everything wishes to live *up to a point.* Past a certain point, and in certain conditions, death becomes preferable to life. Moreover, it was generally agreed that a good life was preferable to one that was merely long, and that the goodness of a life could not be determined by its length. The statisticians of longevity ignore good in both its senses; they do not ask if the prolonged life is virtuous, or if it is satisfactory. If the life is that of a vicious criminal, or if it is inched out in a veritable hell of captivity within the medical industry, no matter—both become statistics to "prove" the good luck of living in our time.

But in general, apart from its own highly specialized standards of quantity and efficiency, "technological progress" has produced a social and ecological decline. Industrial war, except by the most fanatically narrow standards, is worse than war used to be. Industrial agriculture, except by the standards of quantity and mechanical efficiency, diminishes everything it affects. Industrial workmanship is certainly worse than traditional workmanship, and is getting shoddier every day. After forty-odd years, the evidence is everywhere that television, far from proving a great tool of education, is a tool of stupefaction and disintegration. Industrial education has abandoned the old duty of passing on the cultural and intellectual inheritance in favor of baby-sitting and career preparation.

After several generations of "technological progress," in fact, we have become a people who *cannot* think about anything important. How far down in the natural order do we have to go to find creatures who raise their young as indifferently as industrial humans now do? Even the English sparrows do not let loose into the streets young sparrows who have no notion of their identity or their adult responsibilities. When else in history would you find "educated" people who know more about sports than about the history of their country, or uneducated people who do not know the stories of their families and communities?

To ask a still more obvious question, what is the purpose of this technological progress? What higher aim do we think it is serving? Surely the aim cannot be the integrity or happiness of our families, which we have made subordinate to the education system, the television industry, and the consumer economy. Surely it cannot be the integrity or health of our communities, which we esteem even less than we esteem our families. Surely it cannot be love of our country, for we are far more concerned about the desecration of the flag than we are about the desecration of our land. Surely it cannot be the love of God, which counts for at least as little in the daily order of business as the love of family, community, and country.

The higher aims of "technological progress" are money and ease. And this exalted greed for money and ease is disguised and justified by an obscure, cultish faith in "the future." We do as we do, we say, "for the sake of the future" or "to make a better future for our children." How we can hope to make a good future by doing badly in the present, we do not say. We cannot think about the future, of course, for the future does not exist: the existence of the future is an article of faith. We can be assured only that, if there is to be a future, the good of it is already implicit in the good things of the present. We do not need to plan or devise a "world of the future"; if we take care of the world of the present, the future will have received full justice from us. A good future is implicit in the soils, forests, grasslands, marshes, deserts, mountains, rivers, lakes, and oceans that we have now, and in the good things of human culture that we have now; the only valid "futurology" available to us is to take care of those things. We have no need to contrive and dabble at "the future of the human race"; we have the same pressing need that we have always had—to love, care for, and teach our children.

And so the question of the desirability of adopting any technological innovation is a question with two possible answers— not one, as has been commonly assumed. If one's motives are money, ease, and haste to arrive in a technologically determined future, then the answer is foregone, and there is, in fact, no question, and no thought. If one's motive is the love of family, community, country, and God, then one will have to think, and one may have to decide that the proposed innovation is undesirable.

The question of how to end or reduce dependence on some of the technological innovations already adopted is a baffling one. At least, it baffles me. I have not been able to see, for example, how people living in the country, where there is no public transportation, can give up their automobiles without becoming less useful to each other. And this is because, owing largely to the influence of the automobile, we live too far from each other, and from the things we need, to be able to get about by any other means. Of course, you *could* do without an automobile, but to do so you would have to disconnect yourself from many obligations. Nothing I have so far been able to think about this problem has satisfied me.

But if we have paid attention to the influence of the automobile on country communities, we know that the desirability of technological innovation is an issue that requires thinking about, and we should have acquired some ability to think about it. Thus if I am partly a writer, and I am offered an expensive machine to help me write, I ought to ask whether or not such a machine is desirable.

I should ask, in the first place, whether or not I wish to purchase a solution to a problem that I do not have. I acknowledge that, as a writer, I need a lot of help. And I have received an abundance of the best of help from my wife, from other members of my family, from friends, from teachers, from editors, and sometimes from readers. These people have helped me out of love or friendship, and perhaps in exchange for some help that I have given them. I suppose I should leave open the possibility that I need more help than I am getting, but I would certainly be ungrateful and greedy to think so.

But a computer, I am told, offers a kind of help that you can't get from other humans; a computer will help you to write faster, easier, and more. For a while, it seemed to me that every university professor I met told me this. Do I, then, want to write faster, easier, and more? No. My standards are not speed, ease, and quantity. I have already left behind too much evidence that, writing with a pencil, I have written too fast, too easily, and too much. I would like to be a *better* writer, and for that I need help from other humans, not a machine.

The professors who recommended speed, ease, and quantity to me were, of course, quoting the standards of their universities. The chief concern of the industrial system, which is to say the present university system, is to cheapen work by increasing volume. But implicit in the professors' recommendation was the idea that one needs to be up with the times. The pace-setting academic intellectuals have lately had a great hankering to be up with the times. They don't worry about keeping up with the Joneses: as intellectuals, they know that they are supposed to be Nonconformists and Independent Thinkers living at the Cutting Edge of Human Thought. And so they are all a-dither to keep up with the times—which means adopting the latest technological innovations as soon as the Joneses do.

Do I wish to keep up with the times? No.

My wish simply is to live my life as fully as I can. In both our work and our leisure, I think, we should be so employed. And in our time this means that we must save ourselves from the products that we are asked to buy in order, ultimately, to replace ourselves.

The danger most immediately to be feared in "technological progress" is the degradation and obsolescence of the body. Implicit in the technological revolution from the beginning has been a new version of an old dualism, one always destructive, and now more destructive than ever. For many centuries there have been people who looked upon the body, as upon the natural world, as an encumbrance of the soul, and so have hated the body, as they have hated the natural world, and longed to be free of it. They have seen the body as intolerably imperfect by spiritual standards. More recently, since the beginning of the technological revolution, more and more people have looked upon the body, along with the rest of the natural creation, as intolerably imperfect by mechanical standards. They see the body as an encumbrance of the mind—the mind, that is, as reduced to a set of mechanical ideas that can be implemented in machines—and so they hate it and long to be free of it. The body has limits that the machine does not have; therefore, remove the body from the machine so that the machine can continue as an unlimited idea.

It is odd that simply because of its "sexual freedom" our time should be considered extraordinarily physical. In fact, our "sexual revolution" is mostly an industrial phenomenon, in which the body is used as an idea of pleasure or a pleasure machine with the aim of "freeing" natural pleasure from natural consequence. Like any other industrial enterprise, industrial sexuality seeks to conquer nature by exploiting it and ignoring the consequences, by denying any connection between nature and spirit or body and soul, and by evading social responsibility. The spiritual, physical, and economic costs of this "freedom" are immense, and are characteristically belittled or ignored. The diseases of sexual irresponsibility are regarded as a technological problem and an affront to liberty. Industrial sex, characteristically, establishes its freeness and goodness by an industrial accounting, dutifully toting up numbers of "sexual partners," orgasms, and so on, with the inevitable industrial implication that the body is somehow a limit on the idea of sex, which will be a great deal more abundant as soon as it can be done by robots.

This hatred of the body and of the body's life in the natural world, always inherent in the technological revolution (and sometimes explicitly and vengefully so), is of concern to an artist because art, like sexual love, is of the body. Like sexual love, art is of the mind and spirit also, but it is made with the body and it appeals to the senses. To reduce or shortcut the intimacy of the body's involvement in the making of a work of art (that is, of any artifice, anything made by art) inevitably risks reducing the work of art and the art itself. In addition to the reasons I gave previously, which I still believe are good reasons, I am not going to use a computer because I don't want to diminish or distort my bodily involvement in my work. I don't want to deny myself the *pleasure* of bodily involvement in my work, for that pleasure seems to me to be the sign of an indispensable integrity.

At first glance, writing may seem not nearly so much an art of the body as, say, dancing or gardening or carpentry. And yet language is the most intimately physical of all the artistic means. We have it palpably in our mouths; it is our *langue*, our tongue. Writing it, we shape it with our hands. Reading aloud what we have written—as we must do, if we are writing carefully—our language passes in at the eyes, out at the mouth, in at the ears; the words are immersed and steeped in the senses of the body before they make sense in the mind. They *cannot* make sense in the mind until they have made sense in the body. Does shaping one's words with one's own hand impart character and quality to them, as does speaking them with one's own tongue to the satisfaction of one's own ear? There is no way to prove that it does. On the other hand, there is no way to prove that it does not, and I believe that it does.

The act of writing language down is not so insistently tangible an act as the act of building a house or playing the violin. But to the extent that it is tangible, I love the tangibility of it. The computer apologists, it seems to me, have greatly underrated the value of the handwritten manuscript as an artifact. I don't mean that a writer should be a fine calligrapher and write for exhibition, but rather that handwriting has a valuable influence on the work so written. I am certainly no calligrapher, but my handwritten pages have a homemade, handmade look to them that both pleases me in itself and suggests the possibility of ready correction. It looks hospitable to improvement. As the longhand is transformed into typescript and then into galley proofs and the printed page, it seems increasingly to resist improvement. More and more spunk is required to mar the clean, final-looking lines of type. I have the notion—again not provable—that the longer I keep a piece of work in longhand, the better it will be.

To me, also, there is a significant difference between ready correction and easy correction. Much is made of the ease of correction in computer work, owing to the insubstantiality of the light-image on the screen; one presses a button and the old version disappears, to be replaced by the new. But because of the substantiality of paper and the consequent difficulty involved, one does not handwrite or typewrite a new page every time a correction is made. A handwritten or typewritten page therefore is usually to some degree a palimpsest; it contains parts and relics of its own history—erasures, passages crossed out, interlineations—suggesting that there is something to go back to as well as something to go forward to. The light-text on the computer screen, by contrast, is an artifact typical of what can only be called the industrial present, a present absolute. A computer destroys the sense of historical succession, just as do other forms of mechanization. The well-crafted table or cabinet embodies the memory of (because it embodies respect for) the tree it was made of and the forest in which the tree stood. The work of certain potters embodies the memory that the clay was dug from the earth. Certain farms contain hospitably the remnants and reminders of the forest or prairie that preceded them. It is possible even for towns and cities to remember farms and forests or prairies. All good human work remembers its history. The best writing, even when printed, is full of intimations that it is the present version of earlier versions of itself, and that its maker inherited the work and the ways of earlier makers. It thus keeps, even in print, a suggestion of the quality of the handwritten page; it is a palimpsest.

Something of this undoubtedly carries over into industrial products. The plastic Clorox jug has a shape and a loop for the forefinger that recalls the stoneware jug that went before it. But something vital is missing. It embodies no memory of its source or sources in the earth or of any human hand involved in its shaping. Or look at a large factory or a power plant or an airport, and see if you can imagine—even if you know—what was there before. In such things the materials of the world have entered a kind of orphanhood.

It would be uncharitable and foolish of me to suggest that nothing good will ever be written on a computer. Some of my best friends have computers. I have only said that a computer cannot help you to write *better*, and I stand by that. (In fact, I know a publisher who says that under the influence of computers—or of the immaculate copy that computers produce—many writers are now writing worse.) But I do say that in using computers writers are flirting with a radical separation of mind and body, the elimination of the work of the body from the work of the mind. The text on the computer screen, and the computer printout too, has a sterile, untouched, factorymade look, like that of a plastic whistle or a new car. The body does not do work like that. The body *characterizes* everything it touches. What it makes it traces over with the marks of its pulses and breathings, its excitements, hesitations, flaws, and mistakes. On its good work, it leaves the marks of skill, care, and love persisting through hesitations, flaws, and mistakes. And to those of us who love and honor the life of the body in this world, these marks are precious things, necessities of life.

But writing is of the body in yet another way. It is preeminently a walker's art. It can be done on foot and at large. The beauty of its traditional equipment is simplicity. And cheapness. Going off to the woods, I take a pencil and some paper (*any* paper—a small notebook, an old envelope, a piece of a feed sack), and I am as well equipped for my work as the president of IBM. I am also free, for the time being at least, of everything that IBM is hooked to. My thoughts will not be coming to me from the power structure or the power grid, but from another direction and way entirely. My mind is free to go with my feet.

I know that there are some people, perhaps many, to whom you cannot appeal on behalf of the body. To them, disembodiment is a goal, and they long for the realm of pure mind—or pure machine; the difference is negligible. Their departure from their bodies, obviously, is much to be desired, but the rest of us had better be warned: they are going to cause a lot of dangerous commotion on their way out.

Some of my critics were happy to say that my refusal to use a computer would not do any good. I have argued, and am convinced, that it will at least do *me* some good, and that it may involve me in the preservation of some cultural goods. But what they meant was real, practical, public good. They meant that the materials and energy I save by not buying a computer will not be "significant." They meant that no individual's restraint in the use of technology or energy will be "significant." That is true.

But each one of us, by "insignificant" individual abuse of the world, contributes to a general abuse that is devastating. And if I were one of thousands or millions of people who could afford a piece of equipment, even one for which they had a conceivable "need," and yet did not buy it, *that* would be "significant." Why, then, should I hesitate for even a moment to be one, even the first one, of that "significant" number? Thoreau gave the definitive reply to the folly of "significant numbers" a long time ago: Why should anybody wait to do what is right until everybody does it? It is not "significant" to love your own children or to eat your own dinner, either. But normal humans will not wait to love or eat until it is mandated by an act of Congress.

One of my correspondents asked where one is to draw the line. That question returns me to the bewilderment I mentioned earlier: I am unsure where the line ought to be drawn, or how to draw it. But it is an intelligent question, worth losing some sleep over.

I know how to draw the line only where it is easy to draw. It is easy—it is even a luxury—to deny oneself the use of a television set, and I zealously practice that form of self-denial. Every time I see television (at other people's houses), I am more inclined to congratulate myself on my deprivation. I have no doubt, as I have said, that I am better off without a computer. I joyfully deny myself a motorboat, a camping van, an off-road vehicle, and every other kind of recreational machinery. I have, and want, no "second home." I suffer very comfortably the lack of colas, TV dinners, and other counterfeit foods and beverages.

I am, however, still in bondage to the automobile industry and the energy companies, which have nothing to recommend them except our dependence on them. I still fly on airplanes, which have nothing to recommend them but speed; they are inconvenient, uncomfortable, undependable, ugly, stinky, and scary. I still cut my wood with a chainsaw, which has nothing to recommend it but speed, and has all the faults of an airplane, except it does not fly.

It is plain to me that the line ought to be drawn without fail wherever it can be drawn easily. And it ought to be easy (though many do not find it so) to refuse to buy what one does not need. If you are already solving your problem with the equipment you have—a pencil, say—why solve it with something more expensive and more damaging? If you don't have a problem, why pay for a solution? If you love the freedom and elegance of simple tools, why encumber yourself with something complicated?

And yet, if we are ever again to have a world fit and pleasant for little children, we are surely going to have to draw the line where it is *not* easily drawn. We are going to have to learn to give up things that we have learned (in only a few years, after all) to "need." I am not an optimist; I am afraid that I won't live long enough to escape my bondage to the machines. Nevertheless, on every day left to me I will search my mind and circumstances for the means of escape. And I am not without hope. I knew a man who, in the age of chainsaws, went right on cutting his wood with a handsaw and an axe. He was a healthier and a saner man than I am. I shall let his memory trouble my thoughts.

1989

WORD AND FLESH

Toward the end of *As You Like It*, Orlando says: "I can live no longer by thinking." He is ready to marry Rosalind. It is time for incarnation. Having thought too much, he is at one of the limits of human experience, or of human sanity. If his love does put on flesh, we know he must sooner or later arrive at the opposite limit, at which he will say, "I can live no longer without thinking." Thought—even consciousness—seems to live between these limits: the abstract and the particular, the word and the flesh.

All public movements of thought quickly produce a language that works as a code, useless to the extent that it is abstract. It is readily evident, for example, that you can't conduct a relationship with another person in terms of the rhetoric of the civil rights movement or the women's movement—as useful as those rhetorics may initially have been to personal relationships.

The same is true of the environment movement. The favorite adjective of this movement now seems to be "planetary." This word is used, properly enough, to refer to the interdependence of places, and to the recognition, which is desirable and growing, that no place on the earth can be completely healthy until all places are.

But the word "planetary" also refers to an abstract anxiety or an abstract passion that is desperate and useless exactly to the extent that it is abstract. How, after all, can anybody—any particular body—do anything to heal a planet? The suggestion that anybody could do so is preposterous. The heroes of abstraction keep galloping in on their white horses to save the planet—and they keep falling off in front of the grandstand.

What we need, obviously, is a more intelligent—which is to

say, a more accurate—description of the problem. The description of a problem as planetary arouses a motivation for which, of necessity, there is no employment. The adjective "planetary" describes a problem in such a way that it cannot be solved. In fact, though we now have serious problems nearly everywhere on the planet, we have no problem that can accurately be described as planetary. And, short of the total annihilation of the human race, there is no planetary solution.

There are also no national, state, or county problems, and no national, state, or county solutions. That will-o'-the-wisp, the large-scale solution to the large-scale problem, which is so dear to governments, universities, and corporations, serves mostly to distract people from the small, private problems that they may, in fact, have the power to solve.

The problems, if we describe them accurately, are all private and small. Or they are so initially.

`The problems are our lives. In the "developed" countries, at least, the large problems occur because all of us are living either partly wrong or almost entirely wrong.' It was not just the greed of corporate shareholders and the hubris of corporate executives that put the fate of Prince William Sound into one ship; it was also our demand that energy be cheap and plentiful.

The economies of our communities and households are wrong. The answers to the human problems of ecology are to be found in economy. And the answers to the problems of economy are to be found in culture and in character. To fail to see this is to go on dividing the world falsely between guilty producers and innocent consumers.

The planetary versions—the heroic versions—of our problems have attracted great intelligence. But these problems, as they are caused and suffered in our lives, our households, and our communities, have attracted very little intelligence.

There are some notable exceptions. A few people have learned to do a few things better. But it is discouraging to reflect that, though we have been talking about most of our problems for decades, we are still mainly *talking* about them. The civil rights movement has not given us better communities. The women's movement has not given us better marriages or better households. The environment movement has not changed our parasitic relationship to nature.

We have failed to produce new examples of good home and community economies, and we have nearly completed the destruction of the examples we once had. Without examples, we are left with theory and the bureaucracy and meddling that come with theory. We change our principles, our thoughts, and our words, but these are changes made in the air. Our lives go on unchanged.

For the most part, the subcultures, the countercultures, the dissenters, and the opponents continue mindlessly—or perhaps just helplessly—to follow the pattern of the dominant society in its extravagance, its wastefulness, its dependencies, and its addictions. The old problem remains: How do you get intelligence *out* of an institution or an organization?

My small community in Kentucky has lived and dwindled for at least a century under the influence of four kinds of organizations: governments, corporations, schools, and churches—all of which are distant (either actually or in interest), centralized, and consequently abstract in their concerns.

Governments and corporations (except for employees) have no presence in our community at all, which is perhaps fortunate for us, but we nevertheless feel the indifference or the contempt of governments and corporations for communities such as ours.

We have had no school of our own for nearly thirty years. The school system takes our young people, prepares them for "the world of tomorrow"—which it does not expect to take place in any rural area—and gives back "expert" (that is, extremely generalized) ideas.

The church is present in the town. We have two churches. But both have been used by their denominations, for almost a century, to provide training and income for student ministers, who do not stay long enough even to become disillusioned.

For a long time, then, the minds that have most influenced our town have not been *of* the town and so have not tried even to perceive, much less to honor, the good possibilities that are there. They have not wondered on what terms a good and conserving life might be lived there. In this my community is not unique but is like almost every other neighborhood in our country and in the "developed" world.

The question that *must* be addressed, therefore, is not how to care for the planet, but how to care for each of the planet's millions of human and natural neighborhoods, each of its millions of small pieces and parcels of land, each one of which is in some precious way different from all the others. Our understandable wish to preserve the planet must somehow be reduced to the scale of our competence—that is, to the wish to preserve all of its humble households and neighborhoods.

What can accomplish this reduction? I will say again, without overweening hope but with certainty nonetheless, that only love can do it. Only love can bring intelligence out of the institutions and organizations, where it aggrandizes itself, into the presence of the work that must be done.

Love is never abstract. It does not adhere to the universe or the planet or the nation or the institution or the profession, but to the singular sparrows of the street, the lilies of the field, "the least of these my brethren." Love is not, by its own desire, heroic. It is heroic only when compelled to be. It exists by its willingness to be anonymous, humble, and unrewarded.

The older love becomes, the more clearly it understands its involvement in partiality, imperfection, suffering, and mortality. Even so, it longs for incarnation. It can live no longer by thinking.

And yet to put on flesh and do the flesh's work, it must think.

In his essay on Kipling, George Orwell wrote: "All left-wing parties in the highly industrialized countries are at bottom a sham, because they make it their business to fight against something which they do not really wish to destroy. They have internationalist aims, and at the same time they struggle to keep up a standard of life with which those aims are incompatible. We all live by robbing Asiatic coolies, and those of us who are 'enlightened' all maintain that those coolies ought to be set free; but our standard of living, and hence our 'enlightenment,' demands that the robbery shall continue."

This statement of Orwell's is clearly applicable to our situation now; all we need to do is change a few nouns. The religion and the environmentalism of the highly industrialized countries are at bottom a sham, because they make it their business to fight against something that they do not really wish to destroy. We all live by robbing nature, but our standard of living demands that the robbery shall continue.

We must achieve the character and acquire the skills to live much poorer than we do. We must waste less. We must do more for ourselves and each other. It is either that or continue merely to think and talk about changes that we are inviting catastrophe to make.

The great obstacle is simply this: the conviction that we cannot change because we are dependent on what is wrong. But that is the addict's excuse, and we know that it will not do.

How dependent, in fact, are we? How dependent are our neighborhoods and communities? How might our dependences be reduced? To answer these questions will require better thoughts and better deeds than we have been capable of so far.

We must have the sense and the courage, for example, to see that the ability to transport food for hundreds or thousands of miles does not necessarily mean that we are well off. It means that the food supply is more vulnerable and more costly than a local food supply would be. It means that consumers do not control or influence the healthfulness of their food supply and that they are at the mercy of the people who have the control and influence. It means that, in eating, people are using large quantities of petroleum that other people in another time are almost certain to need.

Our most serious problem, perhaps, is that we have become a nation of fantasists. We believe, apparently, in the infinite availability of finite resources. We persist in land-use methods that reduce the potentially infinite power of soil fertility to a finite quantity, which we then proceed to waste as if it were an infinite quantity. We have an economy that depends not on the quality and quantity of necessary goods and services but on the moods of a few stockbrokers. We believe that democratic freedom can be preserved by people ignorant of the history of democracy and indifferent to the responsibilities of freedom.

Our leaders have been for many years as oblivious to the realities and dangers of their time as were George III and Lord North. They believe that the difference between war and peace is still the overriding political difference—when, in fact, the difference has diminished to the point of insignificance. How would you describe the difference between modern war and modern industry—between, say, bombing and strip mining, or between chemical warfare and chemical manufacturing? The difference seems to be only that in war the victimization of humans is directly intentional and in industry it is "accepted" as a "trade-off."

Were the catastrophes of Love Canal, Bhopal, Chernobyl, and the *Exxon Valdez* episodes of war or of peace? They were, in fact, peacetime acts of aggression, intentional to the extent that the risks were known and ignored.

We are involved unremittingly in a war not against "foreign enemies," but against the world, against our freedom, and indeed against our existence. Our so-called industrial accidents should be looked upon as revenges of Nature. We forget that Nature is necessarily party to all our enterprises and that she imposes conditions of her own.

Now she is plainly saying to us: "If you put the fates of whole communities or cities or regions or ecosystems at risk in single ships or factories or power plants, then I will furnish the drunk or the fool or the imbecile who will make the necessary small mistake."

1989

NATURE AS MEASURE

I live in a part of the country that at one time a good farmer could take some pleasure in looking at. When I first became aware of it, in the 1940s, the better land, at least, was generally well farmed. The farms were mostly small and were highly diversified, producing cattle, sheep, and hogs, tobacco, corn, and the small grains; nearly all the farmers milked a few cows for home use and to market milk or cream. Nearly every farm household maintained a garden, kept a flock of poultry, and fattened its own meat hogs. There was also an extensive "support system" for agriculture: every community had its blacksmith shop, shops that repaired harness and machinery, and stores that dealt in farm equipment and supplies.

Now the country is not well farmed, and driving through it has become a depressing experience. Some good small farmers remain, and their farms stand out in the landscape like jewels. But they are few and far between, and they are getting fewer every year. The buildings and other improvements of the old farming are everywhere in decay or have vanished altogether. The produce of the country is increasingly specialized. The small dairies are gone. Most of the sheep flocks are gone, and so are most of the enterprises of the old household economy. There is less livestock and more cash-grain farming. When cash-grain farming comes in, the fences go, the livestock goes, erosion increases, and the fields become weedy.

Like the farm land, the farm communities are declining and eroding. The farmers who are still farming do not farm with as much skill as they did forty years ago, and there are not nearly so many farmers farming as there were forty years ago. As the old have died, they have not been replaced; as the young come of age, they leave farming or leave the community. And as the land and the people deteriorate, so necessarily must the support system. None of the small rural towns is thriving as it did forty years ago. The proprietors of small businesses give up or die and are not replaced. As the farm trade declines, farm equipment franchises are revoked. The remaining farmers must drive longer and longer distances for machines and parts and repairs.

Looking at the country now, one cannot escape the conclusion that there are no longer enough people on the land to farm it well and to take proper care of it. A further and more ominous conclusion is that there is no longer a considerable number of people knowledgeable enough to look at the country and see that it is not properly cared for—though the face of the country is now everywhere marked by the agony of our enterprise of self-destruction.

And suddenly in this wasting countryside there is talk of raising production quotas on Burley tobacco by twenty-four percent, and tobacco growers are coming under pressure from the manufacturers to decrease their use of chemicals. Everyone I have talked to is doubtful that we have enough people left in farming to meet the increased demand for either quantity or quality, and doubtful that we still have the barnroom to house the increased acreage. In other words, the demand going up has met the culture coming down. No one can be optimistic about the results.

Tobacco, I know, is not a food, but it comes from the same resources of land and people that food comes from, and this emerging dilemma in the production of tobacco can only foreshadow a similar dilemma in the production of food. At every point in our food economy, present conditions remaining, we must expect to come to a time when demand (for quantity or quality) going up will meet the culture coming down. The fact is that we have nearly destroyed American farming, and in the process have nearly destroyed our country.

How has this happened? It has happened because of the application to farming of far too simple a standard. For many years, as a nation, we have asked our land only to produce, and we have asked our farmers only to produce. We have believed that this single economic standard not only guaranteed good performance but also preserved the ultimate truth and rightness of our aims. We have bought unconditionally the economists' line that competition and innovation would solve all problems, and that we would finally accomplish a technological end-run around biological reality and the human condition.

Competition and innovation have indeed solved, for the time being, the problem of production. But the solution has been extravagant, thoughtless, and far too expensive. We have been winning, to our inestimable loss, a competition against our own land and our own people. At present, what we have to show for this "victory" is a surplus of food. But this is a surplus achieved by the ruin of its sources, and it has been used, by apologists for our present economy, to disguise the damage by which it was produced. Food, clearly, is the most important economic product—except when there is a surplus. When there is a surplus, according to our present economic assumptions, food is the *least* important product. The surplus becomes famous as evidence to consumers that they have nothing to worry about, that there is no problem, that present economic assumptions are correct.

But our present economic assumptions are failing in agriculture, and to those having eyes to see the evidence is everywhere, in the cities as well as in the countryside. The singular demand for production has been unable to acknowledge the importance of the sources of production in nature and in human culture. Of course agriculture must be productive; that is a requirement as urgent as it is obvious. But urgent as it is, it is not the *first* requirement; there are two more requirements equally important and equally urgent. One is that if agriculture is to remain productive, it must preserve the land, and the fertility and ecological health of the land; the land, that is, must be used *well*. A further requirement, therefore, is that if the land is to be used well, the people who use it must know it well, must be highly motivated to use it well, must know how to use it well, must have time to use it well, and must be able to afford to use it well. Nothing that has happened in the agricultural revolution of the last fifty years has disproved or invalidated these requirements, though everything that has happened has ignored or defied them.

In light of the necessity that the farm land and the farm people should thrive while producing, we can see that the single standard of productivity has failed.

Now we must learn to replace that standard by one that is more comprehensive: the standard of nature. The effort to do this is not new. It was begun early in this century by Liberty Hyde Bailey of the Cornell University College of Agriculture, by F. H. King of the University of Wisconsin College of Agriculture and the United States Department of Agriculture, by J. Russell Smith, professor of economic geography at Columbia University, by the British agricultural scientist Sir Albert Howard, and by others; and it has continued into our own time in the work of such scientists as John Todd, Wes Jackson, and others. The standard of nature is not so simple or so easy a standard as the standard of productivity. The term "nature" is not so definite or stable a concept as the weights and measures of productivity. But we know what we mean when we say that the first settlers in any American place recognized that place's agricultural potential "by its nature"—that is, by the depth and quality of its soil, the kind and quality of its native vegetation, and so on. And we know what we mean when we say that all too often we have proceeded to ignore the nature of our places in farming them. By returning to "the nature of the place" as standard, we acknowledge the necessary limits of our own intentions. Farming cannot take place except in nature; therefore, if nature does not thrive, farming cannot thrive. But we know too that nature includes us. It is not a place into which we reach from some safe standpoint outside it. We are in it and are a part of it while we use it. If it does not thrive, we cannot thrive. The appropriate measure of farming then is the world's health and our health, and this is inescapably *one* measure.

But the oneness of this measure is far different from the singularity of the standard of productivity that we have been using; it is far more complex. One of its concerns, one of the inevitable natural measures, is productivity; but it is also concerned for the health of all the creatures belonging to a given place, from the creatures of the soil and water to the humans and other creatures of the land surface to the birds of the air. The use of nature as measure proposes an atonement between ourselves and our world, between economy and ecology, between the domestic and the wild. Or it proposes a conscious and careful recognition of the interdependence between ourselves and nature that in fact has always existed and, if we are to live, must always exist.

Industrial agriculture, built according to the single standard of productivity, has dealt with nature, including human nature, in the manner of a monologist or an orator. It has not asked for anything, or waited to hear any response. It has told nature what it wanted, and in various clever ways has taken what it wanted. And since it proposed no limit on its wants, exhaustion has been its inevitable and foreseeable result. This, clearly, is a dictatorial or totalitarian form of behavior, and it is as totalitarian in its use of people as it is in its use of nature. Its connections to the world and to humans and the other creatures become more and more abstract, as its economy, its authority, and its power become more and more centralized.

On the other hand, an agriculture using nature, including human nature, as its measure would approach the world in the manner of a conversationalist. It would not impose its vision and its demands upon a world that it conceives of as a stockpile of raw material, inert and indifferent to any use that may be made of it. It would not proceed directly or soon to some supposedly ideal state of things. It *would* proceed directly and soon to serious thought about our condition and our predicament. On all farms, farmers would undertake to know responsibly where they are and to "consult the genius of the place." They would ask what nature would be doing there if no one were farming there. They would ask what nature would permit them to do there, and what they could do there with the least harm to the place and to their natural and human neighbors. And they would ask what nature would *help* them to do there. And after each asking, knowing that nature will respond, they would attend carefully to her response. The use of the place would necessarily change, and the response of the place to that use would necessarily change the user. The conversation itself would thus assume a kind of creaturely life, binding the place and its inhabitants together, changing and growing to no end, no final accomplishment, that can be conceived or foreseen.

Farming in this way, though it certainly would proceed by desire, is not visionary in the political or utopian sense. In a conversation, you always expect a reply. And if you honor the other party to the conversation, if you honor the *otherness* of the other party, you understand that you must not expect always to receive a reply that you foresee or a reply that you will like. A conversation is immitigably two-sided and always to some degree mysterious; it requires faith.

For a long time now we have understood ourselves as traveling toward some sort of industrial paradise, some new Eden conceived and constructed entirely by human ingenuity. And we have thought ourselves free to use and abuse nature in any way that might further this enterprise. Now we face overwhelming evidence that we are not smart enough to recover Eden by assault, and that nature does not tolerate or excuse our abuses. If, in spite of the evidence against us, we are finding it hard to relinquish our old ambition, we are also seeing more clearly every day how that ambition has reduced and enslaved us. We see how everything—the whole world—is belittled by the idea that all creation is moving or ought to move toward an end that some body, some human body, has thought up. To be free of that end and that ambition would be a delightful and precious thing. Once free of it, we might again go about our work and our lives with a seriousness and pleasure denied to us when we merely submit to a fate already determined by gigantic politics, economics, and technology.

Such freedom is implicit in the adoption of nature as the measure of economic life. The reunion of nature and economy proposes a necessary democracy, for neither economy nor nature can be abstract in practice. When we adopt nature as measure, we require practice that is locally knowledgeable. The particular farm, that is, must not be treated as any farm. And the particular knowledge of particular places is beyond the competence of any centralized power or authority. Farming by the measure of nature, which is to say the nature of the particular place, means that farmers must tend farms that they know and love, farms small enough to know and love, using tools and methods that they know and love, in the company of neighbors that they know and love.

In recent years, our society has been required to think again of the issues of the use and abuse of human beings. We understand, for instance, that the inability to distinguish between a particular woman and any woman is a condition predisposing to abuse. It is time that we learn to apply the same understanding to our country. The inability to distinguish between a farm and any farm is a condition predisposing to abuse, and abuse has been the result. Rape, indeed, has been the result, and we have seen that we are not exempt from the damage we have inflicted. Now we must think of marriage.

1989